The
Royal Oak
Affair

The
Royal Oak
Affair

THE SAGA OF
ADMIRAL COLLARD
AND
BANDMASTER BARNACLE

by
Robert Glenton

LEO COOPER · LONDON

First published in Great Britain in 1991 by
LEO COOPER
190 Shaftesbury Avenue, London WC2H 8JL
an imprint of Pen & Sword Books Ltd.
47 Church Street, Barnsley, S. Yorks S70 2AS

A CIP catalogue record for this book
is available from the British Library

ISBN 0 85052 266 8

Typeset by Hewer Text Composition Services, Edinburgh
Printed in Great Britain by
The Redwood Press, Melksham, Wiltshire

CONTENTS

ACKNOWLEDGEMENTS

I would very much like to thank all who have helped me to try to recapture the atmosphere of those splendid days of the late 'Twenties when the clouds were still well below the horizon, and as the girl said, warship decks were meant for dancing on.

I am especially grateful to two fellow authors – Leslie Gardiner who himself has written of the *Royal Oak* courts martial, and who has been most helpful. And to my wife Stella King for her happy co-operation. I would also like to express my obligation to Mr A.E. 'Bill' Barnacle and other members of Bandmaster Barnacle's family, to Mr Viktor Wickman, Director of the Wickman Maritime Collection in Malta, Mr Robert Gieve and to Mr Tom Hartman for his patience. They have all been very kind.

ROBERT GLENTON

FOREWORD

It was the late 1920s and one of those magnificent social affairs that the Royal Navy organized so well – a dance aboard a flagship of the Mediterranean Fleet, which, with considerable justice, regarded itself as the élite of what was still the biggest navy in the world. Invitations were cherished.

Down below in the Admiral's dining room, his distinguished guests were passing the port decanter. On the quarterdeck naval officers in mess dress and their partners danced a foxtrot under the immaculate awnings. A splendid evening altogether. Until the Admiral used a certain swear word!

Incredible as it might seem, that solitary oath laid a trail that put the careers of three senior officers in jeopardy and star-crossed the highest ambition of Admiral Sir Roger Keyes, one of Britain's greatest naval heroes. It involved Parliament and left a red-faced Board of Admiralty to face the mockery of the world's Press and to be the butt of the cartoonists.

That was when King George V raised a bushy eyebrow and stepped in.

I

The Fleet that did not Sail

ALTHOUGH IT WAS SO EARLY in the morning that the sun had not had time to bleach the high stone walls round Malta's Grand Harbour its usual hot, faded yellow of summer, the ancient bastions were crowded with people. So were the windows and balconies of all the houses with any sort of view.

It was Thursday, 8 June, 1837 and on the still waters the Fleet lay at anchor – *Rodney, Caledonia, Asia, Vanguard, Russell, Ceylon, Rapid, Nautilus*, the cutter *Hind* and, sign of the times, the three still strangely unfamiliar steam vessels *Hedea, Spitfire* and *Firefly*. But all those watching faces on shore had eyes only for a single, small boat being rowed solemnly from HMS *Ceylon* towards HMS *Rodney*. In its sternsheets, under close guard, was a young marine. Private Thomas McSweeney, aged 23, was being taken from his cell to be hanged.

The silence was so intense that when the boat pulled alongside *Rodney* in mid-harbour the voice of the Captain, as he stood by the port gangway and read the death warrant, carried across the placid water and could be heard hundreds of yards away.

Those on shore could clearly see McSweeney being led forward to the hammock netting under the foreyard and watch the noose being put around his neck. The rope, reeved through a block at the yardarm, led aft to where it was manned by McSweeney's fellow Marines and by two seamen from every ship in harbour.

The Captain finished reading the death warrant, a signal gun cracked out, unnaturally loud in the morning hush, and poor McSweeney was

3

promptly hoisted over sixty feet into the air. His body hung at the yardarm for half an hour before the shocked inhabitants of Malta could retrieve and bury it in the cemetery of St Lawrence on the outskirts of Vittoriosa, one of the three old cities on the edge of Grand Harbour. For most years since then the Maltese have tended that grave and kept a candle burning.

McSweeney was an illiterate Irishman who had left home with a record of petty crime. What offence had led him to the yardarm? He had been caught slinging his hammock below when he should have been on deck. His sergeant reported him. McSweeney was in a rage. He waited until the sergeant's back was turned, ran forward and gave him a push. His victim fell only a matter of six feet or so into the waist of the ship, but it was enough to cause his death.

Corporal John Robinson, giving evidence at the court martial, said that McSweeney shouted as he pushed, 'You bugger, I have got my satisfaction now'.

It was the same oath, again directed at a Marine, that was to be heard at least once more and create another sensation in the history of Grand Harbour.

On Sunday, 11 March, 1928, the crowds gathered again on Grand Harbour's ramparts to watch the Fleet. It was a great occasion. The Mediterranean Fleet was due to put to sea at four in the afternoon to join the Atlantic Fleet which had sailed from England. It was the season for the Combined Spring Exercises, the greatest occasion in the Royal Navy's year. After the exercises were over the Atlantic Fleet would return home but the crews of the Malta-based ships had a much brighter prospect before them. They would cruise on to ports in the South of France and Spain to show the flag and exchange hospitality with shore-bound dignitaries – a time of endless parties, dances and general festivity.

Although 1928 was a year when all the talk was of naval disarmament, the Mediterranean Fleet was still a magnificent sight as it prepared to sail. There were the eight mighty battleships of the First Battle Squadron led by HMS *Queen Elizabeth*, of 27,500 tons and eight fifteen-inch guns, and flagship of the Commander-in-Chief, Admiral Sir Roger Keyes, Bart, KCB, KCVO, CMG, DSO, *Warspite*, *Valiant*, *Barham*, *Royal Oak*, *Royal Sovereign*, *Ramillies* and *Resolution*. They were ageing giants, but most had had a complete refit and the others were waiting their turn.

Then there were the eight powerful cruisers of the First and Third Cruiser Squadrons headed by the flagships *Frobisher* and *Cardiff*. There should have been a ninth cruiser with them but *Castor* had been sent on

4

temporary duty to the China station. One more cruiser, the *Cairo*, was flagship ruling the First, Second, Third and Fourth Destroyer Flotillas – thirty-two destroyers in all, not to mention the *Wolsey* and *Woolston* who lay in reserve.

There were the two huge aircraft carriers *Courageous* and *Eagle*, and the nine submarines of the First Submarine Flotilla, plus eight mine-sweepers, the hospital ship *Maine*, with her white-painted hull in dazzling contrast to the immaculate pale grey of the fighting fleet, the survey ship *Endeavour*, two sloops, *Chrysanthemum* and *Bryony*. *Bryony* was not a sloop at all for service purposes but had been extensively converted as the Commander-in-Chief's personal yacht. Add a minelayer, two trawlers and three humble drifters with pleasantly unwarlike names, *Crescent Moon*, *Sunset* and *Landfall*, not to mention a depot ship, oilers and water carriers and there was not a creek from Sliema and Lazaretto, from French Creek to the dockyard, not a buoy in all the broad expanse of Marsamxett Harbour and Grand Harbour that was not occupied, not a berth uncrowded, until one wondered by what ingenuity of seamanship so many vessels had arrived there in the first place. And over all, at six tall mastheads, flew the personal ensigns of half-a-dozen admirals of assorted seniority.

It was a superb scene, unrepeatable anywhere in the world today. Immaculate awnings tautly spread over a hundred quarterdecks, impeccable decks scrubbed almost as white as the awnings that shaded them, peerless paintwork, gleaming tampions in all the great guns' muzzles, each with the heraldic crest of the ship that bore them, a gleam that was repeated a thousand times or more by the polished brasswork of every single item that the Navy could find a hand to polish. And it was not short of hands.

From time to time peremptory bugle calls rang out across the harbour and there was the endless high shrill of bosuns' pipes. Between the ships, in a never-ending flurry, motor boats darted, arrowing the still waters with their wakes, stiff-backed bow and sternsheet ratings performing their faultless drill. On the fo'c'sles of all these ships officers and men were gathering, preparing to unshackle from the mooring buoys and run home the anchor cables. It was an anxious time for them, just as it was for those about to ascend the bridge. Extricating such a large fleet from the narrow limits of Malta's anchorage called for fine seamanship if there was to be no scraped paintwork.

Soon the harbour tugs, already with steam up, would be fussing their way on to the scene to lend a hand. No wonder that half Malta was lining the ramparts to watch. For a few weeks the island was going to seem very lonely with no navy to throng its narrow streets and crowd its harbour.

There were officers' wives and girlfriends; there were prostitutes who were about to have considerable time on their hands; there were owners of bars whose beaded, flyscreen-curtained doorways would not tinkle for some time to come to the entry of thirsty sailors seeking salvation. But most of all the audience around the harbours and the creeks consisted of the ordinary sunburnt Maltese to whom the sailing of the entire Mediterranean Fleet on Spring Exercises was as fine a spectacle as any of their beloved firework displays or religious processions.

Four o'clock in the afternoon came – and with it the impossible. Not a ship stirred. The Almighty decrees the rising and setting of the sun. The Commander-in-Chief Mediterranean decides for himself what those times should be for the purposes of ceremonial. He also dictates when his fleet shall sail. It is Admiralty immutable. And it had been announced by Sir Roger Keyes himself that the Fleet would be sailing at four o'clock. Yet not a quarterdeck awning had been furled and already the unshackling parties had melted from every fo'c'sle. Even the busy motorboats on their errands from ship to ship and ship to shore had disappeared. The Fleet was as silent and as still as the calm waters on which it floated.

For quite a while the spectators lingered, the seawise naval wives and the islanders all wondering. The whole of the Spring Exercise programme depended on the Mediterranean and Atlantic Fleets joining each other on time. What had happened? But night falls quickly in Malta and gradually the crowds drifted away.

Malta has always been famous for its silverware, monks, fireworks, goats and lace, but when Nelson and the Royal Navy arrived a new element was added to its reputation – gossip – gossip about promotion, adultery, other officers' money, or the lack of it, all the ingredients that go to make for a most satisfactory cocktail party, a tea-table chat or a sleepy after-picnic murmur when sprawled on some hot Maltese beach.

That Sunday night when the fleet failed to sail, gossip excelled itself. There was no newspaper to buy in order to seek the reason and the few officers and ratings who managed to get ashore were no help at all. They were just as bewildered. So word of mouth had to do instead. And what word of mouth! Lack of facts has never yet done the least harm to a rumour.

Yet during that Sunday there had been clues. The cross of St George with its two red balls denoting that she was the flagship of Rear-Admiral Bernard St George Collard, CB, DSO, no longer flew at the masthead of the battleship *Royal Oak*. Moreover, a launch had been seen leaving the side of the ship and heading for the shore. Aboard were two silent men wearing civilian suits and trilby hats. They had their luggage with them. They were Captain Kenneth Dewar, CBE, Commanding Officer of the ship, and his second-in-command, Commander Henry Daniel, DSO.

As the night lengthened three theories flourished: there had been a mutiny aboard *Royal Oak*; Rear-Admiral Collard had been ordered ashore in disgrace; there had been a secret court martial.

And all the time the great fleet, which by now should have been many sea miles away, lay below in Grand Harbour, utterly mute. Its anchor lamps burned bright, its quiet quarterdecks were well illuminated, the reflection of hundreds of cabin lights danced in the ripples of the dark water. What exactly had happened aboard *Royal Oak*? Never had the Royal Navy been a more silent service.

Royal Marine Bandmaster Percy Barnacle of that ship could have told them. Indeed he eventually did tell an eagerly listening and incredulous world. For he was to be a central witness in one of the most remarkable courts martial the Royal Navy has ever held: The Case of the Incompatible Flag Officer . . . or what exactly did the Admiral call the leader of the band?

Next day when Malta awoke, drew back its curtains, opened its shutters and stuck its head out of the window, there was another sensation. Grand Harbour was deserted! The Mediterranean Fleet had sailed in the early morning.

In 1928 Malta was a very splendid place. Nowadays it is a charming, even romantic island, very largely dependent on tourism and something of a backwater in the world's affairs. Not so in 1928. For many years before that the Royal Navy had made it its own and every passing decade brought it growing prosperity. Until the Navy came, Malta, ardently and fiercely Roman Catholic, had made its way by fishing and local industry and lived, comparatively poor but contented, amid the crumbling magnificence of its history. For an island measuring only seventeen miles by nine it has a lot to show. Conquered in turn by Phoenicians, Greeks, Carthaginians, Romans and Arabs, it fell to the French less than thirty years after William the Norman fought the Battle of Hastings and took the throne of England. Early in the sixteenth century the French handed

7

the island over to the Knights of St John as a stronghold of Christianity. The Knights, who came from countries all over Europe, were a militant lot in those troublesome times. The sun-bleached bastions on which the crowds gathered in 1928 to watch the fleet that refused to sail were the same formidable defences which the Knights of St John had built. For the Knights knew that trouble would come. Each nation housed its members by building imposing auberges and, to make sure no knight would be so errant as to wander off to Italy for a short holiday, laid down a strict rule that every member of the order should dine in his auberge at least four times a week.

It was a wise precaution, for trouble soon came in the shape of the Turks, determined to destroy the infidels for ever. After an exceedingly bloody campaign the Turks gave the Knights of St John best and sailed home. For over two hundred years thereafter Malta was at peace. But, as every general knows, one cannot keep a standing army on the alert indefinitely. The Knights of St John either merged into the countryside, building themselves handsome palaces (any reasonably large house, preferably with a couple of shady trees in its garden, can be a palace in Malta) or they went home and sent their sons to serve in their place. It was an amicable arrangement that suited both the Knights and the Maltese. Unfortunately Napoleon spoilt it. He had a war on his hands and doubted the ability of the Knights to defend what was, after all, a keystone to the defence of the Mediterranean. So he expelled the lot and replaced them with units of his conscript army.

The islanders took grave umbrage. The Maltese language has elements of everything from French to Arabic and nowadays the way the islanders cheerfully watch and listen to Italian mainland television programmes shows clearly that they have endured, assimilated and finally tolerated a number of conquerors and strange tongues in their history. But they are quite capable of turning nasty. In hardly any time they threw the French army off the island. By a happy coincidence, or so it would seem, the British Navy happened to be on hand. If the Maltese could not have their knights then they would have the British. So a treaty was signed. The British would protect Malta on condition that all the island's rights and privileges were preserved.

In 1928 the agreement was still working well. It is true that even the wealthy and well-born Maltese rarely mixed socially with the British establishment except on such formal occasions as anniversary dinners, balls and the like, but there was a happy prosperity that no one wanted to disturb. There was work in the dockyards and the Maltese earned good pay for learning new skills. From the boatmen in their brightly painted gondola-like dghajjes who attended the fleet in harbour to the swarthy drivers of the horse-drawn gharries ready to taxi any eager group of sailors wherever their spirits, or their thirsty search for spirits, took them, Malta was living well in 1928.

The Mediterranean Fleet regarded itself with some justification as not only the finest force in the British Navy but in any other navy, and Malta was its home, somewhere to relax, take off its boots, put on its carpet slippers and ease its tie. There was astonishingly little discord.

Take Strait Street in Valletta, for example. Cobbled and steeply sloping, it runs its long and narrow way down to the waterfront. Virtually every house on either side was a brothel, a garish bar or a place of dubious entertainment. The Navy loved it, christened it The Gut and reminisced over it from Singapore to Plymouth. The prostitutes could be quite appalling. They were cheap, that goes without saying considering a rating's pay. Many a pink-cheeked Ordinary Seaman who had recently joined the fleet lost his virginity, his wrist watch and the signet ring his girlfriend had given him to some shockingly experienced and wrinkled hag. Now the owner of a blinding hangover, the despair of all the naval surgeons who had exhausted themselves lecturing him and his fellows on the perils of such goings-on and finally having missed the last liberty boat back to his ship, he would find himself paraded before authority and sentenced to seven days' loss of pay. Comforted by his messmates, another member of The Gut had been initiated.

There was astonishingly little violence. True there would be the occasional cheerful melée between sailors and the British military garrison, or between the crews of rival ships, but naval shore patrols, gaiters and belts spotlessly pipeclayed, were always close by ready to lend a heavy, horny and impartial hand should things become too unruly.

While all this was going on and only the width of a short alley away, the Maltese would be crowding the equally steep and narrow thoroughfare of Kingsway which ran parallel, spilling out of the shops and cafés that never seemed to close, or crowding round the gas-lantern-lit stalls at the City Gate. And, more than likely, through the throng would come a slow procession of priests followed by barefooted worshippers, men, women, children, counting their beads and escorted by an echelon of dogs of no known breed. There would be candles, heavily embroidered banners and an even heavier shoulder-borne litter swaying with the weight of the huge

9

effigy of some saint or other. Just as possibly, in the slender gaps in the clear Mediterranean sky that could be seen between the tall buildings, fireworks would burst into dazzling light.

One thing was certain. In 1928 the Maltese and the British Navy shared the island in harmony and rarely trespassed on the other's good nature.

Not all the sailors sought out the garish entertainment of The Gut. There were other traditional haunts where pleasure was taken more seriously. The Navy had established its pubs and the Maltese had happily co-operated. The island even brewed its own beer. Few of these bars were custom-built. Often they were little more than the converted front parlours of waterfront cottages. Yet they became as much of a home-from-home to sailors and petty officers of the Mediterranean Fleet as ever a 'Rose and Crown' or 'Dog and Partridge' back in England.

On Valletta waterfront were the 'Iron Duke', 'The Dreadnought', 'The Ramillies' and 'The City of London'. Maltese landlords knew a thing or two about a name that would catch the customers.

In practically all these taverns you would see on the wall a large wooden panel just like the honours board in any golf club. The inscriptions, floridly painted by some fine Maltese hand, started at the top in a modest sort of way – 'June 26, 1924, Yeoman of Signals R.J. Smith, HMS *Resolution*, consumed 18 Blues between the hours of 5pm and 8pm.' (Blue was the name of the local beer and came in bottles of something over a pint – and note the delicate use of the word 'consumed').

Each subsequent entry would cast a shadow over Yeoman Smith's feat and, worse still, the honour of his ship, until one's eyes fell on the latest: 'November 8, 1927, Chief Petty Officer Brown, HMS *Warspite*, consumed 27 Blues between the hours of 6pm and 10pm.'

It was astonishing how often the local record seemed to be held by a fairly senior petty officer. It must have had something to do with spreading waistlines and experience, certainly not because they earned more pay. Any ordinary seaman showing a trace of form would be sponsored by his messmates, if only for the honour of the ship in which he served. It was the cherished dream of the lower deck of many a flagship to have her name emblazoned proudly on every bar board in Malta.

There was a small problem concerning those who attempted to scale the giddy heights of fame but slipped under the table. The Navy was very tolerant of such goings on. So long as a man could return on board and make a passing semblance of a salute to the quarterdeck, and even if he seemed to be rather closely attended by one or two shipmates, rarely was an eyebrow raised. The theory was that there was no agony that the Lords of the Admiralty could devise that would in any way match that of the culprit when he was invited to show a leg early the next morning.

But for those who could not pass even this simple test there was an answer – the lodging house on Valletta waterfront. It was very popular and called 'The Golden Fleet'. And so it was to its owner's pocket.

There were other, healthier aspects to Jack's life ashore. In the afternoons boisterous and partisan cricket and football matches were played on arid and dusty sports grounds between rival ships and rival services – and against the Maltese, who were no great shakes at cricket but who turned out to be demons at this splendid British game of kicking. For the less active and more imaginative there was a quiet, painful and sometimes bitterly regretted retreat to one of Valletta's tattoo artists.

That was how one part of the Royal Navy lived in Malta.

Life was entirely different for officers. For them it was a unique and prized appointment. First, the Mediterranean Fleet boasted of its supremacy over every other arm of the Navy, a boast that was not entirely without justification. Secondly, it was a station where even an officer with little to live on but his pay could afford to take his wife. Rented accommodation was cheap and convenient and with care, expenses could be kept to a minimum; while his richer shipmates could live in high style with fine accommodation, private gardens for the young children and servants easily available. Some even imported English nannies. The climate was pleasant and travelling was easy. In the days before airliners, Malta was a calling point for all the big passenger ships heading east by way of the Suez Canal. There were arrivals and departures almost every day and in an emergency there was always the overland express across Italy.

Many a young naval wife who could never have afforded to follow her husband to China or the West Indies was happy to put up with three or four days of mild discomfort travelling third class in some liner.

Not that the Admiralty altogether approved of such wives. There were still those who swore by the old saying that junior officers should never marry, commanders ought to and captains must. But in their hearts they knew they were beaten. The Great War, which had ended only ten years before, had seen to that.

Naval wives were not the only feminine company on the island. There were plenty of unattached, attractive and well-born girls who arrived with companions ostensibly on long holidays or to visit relatives in the Fleet, but who were not entirely unaware of the prospects of marriage with so many eligible young men available. The Navy eyed these visitors with cheerful cynicism and called them the fishing fleet.

And there were some fine fish. Not only were many of the most promising young officers in the Royal Navy appointed to the Mediterranean Fleet but also many of the richest. Not a few also had titles. On that Sunday in March, 1928, when the Fleet failed to sail there were serving in it one marquess, one viscount, three lords, three baronets, eight knights and seven honourables. In the flagship *Queen Elizabeth* alone there were two lords, a baronet, an honourable and three knights. True, in this miniature Debrett, most of the knights were long-married senior officers and some of the honourables were young midshipmen, but the prospects were always promising. So were the opportunities to meet them.

Virtually every evening one warship or another would hold a dance or a cocktail party. Many a debutante newly out from home was firmly convinced that the sole purpose of a battleship was to dance on. There were race meetings, picnics and the Opera House. This was Malta's pride and very elegant it was too. Famous Italian singers appeared on its stage from time to time and a gala night or a masked ball, with all the naval officers attending in their mess dress, gold braid and white-lined boat cloaks, was a magnificent spectacle.

Even more impressive were the balls at the Governor's palace. The ballroom itself was lined with suits of armour and ancient weapons, all gleamingly polished and shining under the lights hanging from the superbly painted ceiling. And just to show that the Navy didn't have a monopoly of the island, the Army would be there too in scarlet mess jackets or dress kilts. Between dances there would be the cool of the shady courtyard and, with any luck, a full moon.

More prosaic perhaps but quite as important in the social life of Malta was the Union Club. It had originally been the auberge of the crusading knights of Florence and was in Kingsway, almost within hailing distance of The Gut. It was made a club in 1826 and Sir Walter Scott and Benjamin Disraeli became honorary members. No woman was allowed near the place until 1907 when they were allowed in by a back door, 'so that they would be quite cut off and would not in any way interfere with the comfort and privacy of members'. Her Royal Highness the Duchess of Connaught expressed her outrage at such masculine arrogance and in 1910 women were admitted through a door in the front of the building, but still, in 1928, only to the Ladies' Room. At least they were better off than the Maltese who were not allowed any sort of membership at all.

For all its comfort and its painted Venuses on its ceiling, several views were held about the Ladies' Room. Down below in the Lower Bar, and a very long bar it was, naval officers referred to it as the snake pit and swore that many an honest sailor's career had been poisoned by the gossip that went on upstairs. Most men would only climb those stairs at the behest of their wives, fiancées or girlfriends. Even some young women were not exactly enamoured of the place. Too much of the horse-faced aristocracy, they said. Be that as it may, the Union Club made a comfortable, even vital, meeting place for naval officers and their women.

Most officers who wished to go ashore were entitled to stay there until the Fleet stirred itself in the very early morning. There was a prairie oyster bar at Custom House Steps where raw eggs and Worcester sauce were mixed with great industry until well after midnight for those officers who felt they could do with a tonic before returning to their ships and a reasonably early night.

Married officers usually slept ashore. There was an area known as Snob Hill by the younger naval wives, because the wealthier Britons lived there. Junior wives lived for the most part in rented accommodation round about, in homes with high ceilings, cool stone floors, sparsely furnished, but in the narrow shaded gardens blue larkspur and heavy-scented phlox thrived. The flat-roofed houses overlooked the blue waters of such places as Scaramanga Creek from where the rattle of an anchor cable could be clearly heard, the throb of a submarine recharging its batteries and every evening at sunset the wistful sound of 'Sunset' bugles.

Dancing and gaiety, sunshine and beaches, a friendly island and a superb reputation, the Mediterranean Fleet should have been exceedingly happy. Yet it was not – not entirely.

2

'Staff Work Run Mad'

THE BLAME FOR MUCH OF THE DISCONTENT must sit squarely on the shoulders of the Commander-in-Chief, Mediterranean Fleet, Admiral Sir Roger Keyes.

Keyes was a remarkable man. He was absorbed by his family tree which, he claimed, led in a direct line from the Norman Conquest. His father had been a general, his mother the sister of a field-marshal. Almost from the moment that he entered the Navy as a cadet he seemed determined to prove himself the greatest Keyes of them all. As a junior officer he barged his way forward through the ranks of his fellows. He made a point of being the first to volunteer for any situation that promised danger and distinction. If being the first to volunteer did not always succeed in furthering his plans, he was quite capable of disobeying orders and embarking on the adventure on his own account. For a while he walked the tightrope between disgrace and honour. He was alternately arousing the fury of his senior officers or gaining their reluctant admiration. If he had decided to go into business nowadays he would certainly have ended up as the most sensational bankrupt or a man of great wealth.

As it happened his luck held. But it was not only luck. He often displayed great physical courage. Most certainly he was not popular with many of his contemporaries. In their eyes he was brash and, worse still, a pusher. But his superiors respected his ability, his enterprise and his seamanship. Promotion came fast. He was elevated in rank years before those fellow cadets with whom he had once served.

Then came the First World War and his qualities of audacity, enterprise and, above all, success made him a national hero. It was even suggested that he should be awarded the Victoria Cross, but he never received it. Keyes' father had also been nominated for the medal in his time, equally unsuccessfully. However, a Victoria Cross was eventually awarded to the Keyes family in the Second World War. Keyes' son, Major Geoffrey Keyes, won it when leading a commando raid on Field-Marshal Rommel's headquarters in North Africa. Sadly it was a posthumous award.

In 1919 Sir Roger Keyes was in an unassailable position so far as the Navy was concerned. His reputation was unchallengeable. He had made enemies on his way to the top but now they were unimportant. He had also made some powerful friendships. One, in particular, was with Admiral of the Fleet Earl Beatty, who held the Navy's supreme appointment as First Sea Lord. Apart from the Navy, they shared another common interest – horses. Both were fanatical about hunting and polo. In fact Beatty had once put the hunting season before his career. Had the situation arisen, there is little doubt that Keyes would have done the same.

In May, 1925, at the surprisingly young age of fifty-two, Keyes became Commander-in-Chief, Mediterranean Fleet, a post commonly regarded as second only to Beatty's. He took with him his wife, his young daughters and three polo ponies. He tried to have the ponies transported to Malta aboard a warship but eventually had to settle for a merchantman. He had, incidentally, proposed marriage to his future wife several times without success and was finally accepted on the way back from a morning's hunting.

Polo became something of a fetish in Malta. Keyes himself played almost every day, Lady Keyes and her daughters formed themselves into a team called the Bunch of Keyes and many a socially ambitious young woman who felt that acceptance at Admiralty House was by way of a ladder of polo saddles started wearing jodhpurs.

Young officers, if not exactly expected to play, were certainly given every encouragement. For it was Keyes' firmly held belief that the dash and spirit learnt on the polo ground were the finest possible training for life in a warship.

Some of the officers took happily to the new regime. Others resented the preoccupation with horses and the chaffing it aroused in the rest of the Navy. For legends of the new regime in the Mediterranean spread fast. One young officer appointed to the Fleet is said to have reported on board his ship with a polo mallet under one arm and a copy of Debrett under the other. This story has been repeated so many times in the written reminscences of officers who served in the Mediterranean at the time that it seems highly likely to be true. And unquestionably the periodical publication of promotions soon, and rather sourly, became known as 'Polo promotions'.

There was one ambitious and hard-riding officer who highly approved of all this horseyness. He was Lieutenant-Commander Lord Louis Mountbatten, signals and wireless telegraphy officer aboard HMS *Stuart*, leader of the Second Destroyer Flotilla. Earlier on, Mountbatten, having married into a great deal of money, had been posted to a naval signal school where he had arrived in a spanking new Rolls Royce on which the car's famous bonnet mascot had been replaced at Mountbatten's behest by the gilded figure of a bluejacket holding semaphore flags. His contemporaries, hard-pressed to afford small sports cars, regarded the Rolls Royce as downright ostentatious and the mascot as unspeakably vulgar. This made not a scrap of difference to Mountbatten and by the time he left the school he had written a manual on signalling that was used by the Navy for a long time afterwards. Now he was in Malta, playing polo day after day, and was soon to write a textbook on that subject too.

Mountbatten was the type of officer who warmed Keyes' heart – titled, capable and enterprising, and, like himself, not always popular.

There is no doubt at all that the polo set, and the growing throng of Admiralty House's titled intimates, was irksome to many senior officers and commanders of ships in the Fleet. But there was no quarrel with Keyes himself. He was a sailor's sailor and had proved it over and over again.

The Commander-in-Chief was no orator. More often than not he was completely tongue-tied. He was known to board a ship in harbour, mount a well-burnished and newly painted capstan, survey the assembled officers and men before him, pause for an interminable time, give a few quite incoherent grunts, shuffle off the capstan and disappear. He was loved for it. Action not words was his reputation.

Keyes revelled in his new appointment. He was forever writing copious letters inviting friends and acquaintances, usually influential, to come and holiday on the island and share his pleasures. Bridgeman, the First Lord of the Admiralty, and Beatty, the First Sea Lord, were asked. His future King and Queen, the Duke and Duchess of York, paid a visit. The Duke played polo. Keyes even suggested that Winston Churchill should borrow his official yacht, the converted sloop *Bryony*, for a cruise.

That yacht was one of his particular joys. He would often sail in her in company with the Fleet, taking along as many of his family and friends as the accommodation would allow. Unfortunately she rolled like a tub!

Keyes was happy and, as a man, he was popular. It was his method of command that caused the trouble in the Mediterranean Fleet, particularly his belief in delegation. No Commander-in-Chief of a force the size of the Mediterranean Fleet can attend to even every major detail. He must have men around him who can be trusted. And who better than old allies? Not long after he was appointed as Commander-in-Chief Keyes wrote to one of them, John ('Joe') Kelly, and invited him to become his second-in-command. Kelly answered by saying how much he would like the job but that in all honesty he had to point out that he knew absolutely nothing about handling a fleet or of fleet tactics. Besides that, he was inarticulate and could not put two words together. 'One word,' he wrote, 'then a splutter and then – nothing.' This latter failing was hardly likely to deter Keyes. He persuaded Kelly to join him.

These two men surrounded themselves with a highly efficient staff. Far too efficient perhaps, for it led to a bureaucracy of which the Civil Service would have been proud and to endless paperwork. The Fleet was bombarded with every conceivable form of written order accounting for almost every moment in a ship's working day. Daily reports and returns were demanded for the most trivial reasons. As one captain said wryly, the only decision left to him was what to eat for breakfast! Men brought up to exercise their initiative in command found all this irritating and that irritation was bound to affect their harassed subordinates. A couple of years later a new Commander-in-Chief was to survey the Malta scene and describe it as 'Staff work run mad'. But no guest attending those dances and cocktail parties ever realized this. The Mediterranean Fleet always wore a bland and hospitable expression.

It was in this atmosphere that, around Christmas, 1927, Rear-Admiral Collard, Captain Dewar and Commander Daniel, virtual strangers to each other, joined *Royal Oak* and soon afterwards the officers of the ship decided that they would hold a dance. So began a farce that was to bring a deep blush to the Navy's face, a farce that became a tragedy for one promising officer, blighted the career of another, wrecked that of a third, smeared several others and even destroyed the ambitions of the Commander-in-Chief himself; and left one entirely innocent man with a sense of remorse that he would never forget. That man was Percy Barnacle, Royal Marine Bandmaster 1st Class.

3

Royal Oak Requests the Pleasure

IT WAS IN DECEMBER, 1927, that Collard, Dewar and Daniel met aboard *Royal Oak*. Save that somewhere in the past Dewar and Daniel had spent a few days in the same ship, the men had never served together. Bandmaster Barnacle had been a member of the ship's company for some time.

Collard had only recently been promoted to the rank of rear-admiral and this was his first flag command. It was a post with a minimum of responsibility, for the First Battle Squadron was so well drilled, so highly organized, so well greased and oiled, that there would be scant authority for a new flag officer to exercise. But it was good blooding for real power later.

Collard, the son of a Dorset parson, was 51 years old when he was piped aboard his new flagship on 13 November, 1927. He looked every short inch the part of a senior naval officer. He might have been small in stature but he was very stocky. His dark hair was beginning to thin. Over a nose as sharp as a sparrow's beak his blue eyes were keen. His early days had been spent in sail and he had a bellow of a voice and a vivid vocabulary to prove it. He liked his eating and drinking. He could be sociable and amiably bluff, but owned a notoriously testy temper.

There was, however, much more to him than that. When he first went to sea the Royal Navy's god was paint and polish. The discovery of a new formula for a hard-drying enamel was, at the very least, just as important as the invention of the torpedo. There were even tales told, with considerable evidence to back them, that warships sent to sea on firing exercises would dump their ammunition over the side rather than have the gun barrels scorched and blistered.

It was a situation that could not last, though at first only a few of the brighter young officers realized it. These few saw that promotion and advancement would come only through specialization. Merely to be a good seaman and a supervisor of brass-polishing was not enough. The subject they chose was the much-scorned gunnery, and they were to be proved right. Their star ascended with the coming of the First World War. So did their careers.

Collard was intelligent enough to be one of these junior officers. He studied hard and learnt his subject. He passed each course with distinction.

But one of his first distinctions was not happy. While serving as an instructor lieutenant at Whale Island, known throughout the Navy by the slogan 'Gas, guns and gaiters', he was supervising a party of seamen when it began to rain heavily. The men broke ranks and ran for cover. Angrily Collard called them back and shouted the order, 'On the knee'. The men returned to their places and knelt – all save one seaman who refused.

'On the knee, you dirty dog,' demanded Collard. There, in the rain, the man submitted.

The incident had been noticed and Collard was charged with administering an unauthorized punishment and court-martialled. His defence was that the order 'on the knee' was a traditional command, hallowed in old instructional manuals and merely designed to give an officer a clear view of his mens' faces. Knowing Collard's assiduity in his studies, the Court found it hard to doubt his evidence, though older officers swore that they had never heard of the order. In the end Collard was found guilty and sentenced to be reprimanded. Even such light censure could mar an officer's career, but it did Collard little harm and brought virtually no frown from the Admiralty. It certainly earned him a reputation of sorts. Years later the wife of a future admiral who met him in Gibraltar referred to him as 'that peppery little "On the knee" Collard'.

There was no disputing the man's courage. As a young midshipman he had earned a testimonial from the Royal Humane Society for saving a seaman from drowning. At one stage during the First World War he had been a beachmaster on 'W' Beach at Cape Helles, in the Dardanelles. While any sane man leaves the perils of an invasion beach as rapidly as the situation will allow, Collard's duty was to remain there. And that he did until he was wounded. He returned from the bloody enterprise with a permanent limp and wearing the ribbon of the Distinguished Service Order.

So, on a November Saturday morning in 1927 the Royal Navy's latest and newest flag officer boarded the massive battleship, HMS *Royal Oak*, specially scrubbed and immaculate for the occasion.

The moment that he set foot on deck the symbol of his new authority, a crisp white flag bearing the scarlet cross of St George with its two scarlet balls, was hoisted; the silver bo's'ns' calls twittered and shrilled, echoing from Grand Harbour's walls and battlements.

A moment that any man would treasure. Surely so. But as Collard surveyed Kenneth Dewar, his new Flag Captain, standing stiffly to attention, his sleeve with its four gold rings at the salute, was there a flaw to the moment, a distinct bluebottle in the jam? Very likely. For Rear-Admiral Collard had an acute sense of what was proper. By custom, every flag officer was allowed to choose his own staff – his flag lieutenant, secretaries and communications officers. Above all, he had a say in the choice of his right-hand man, his flag captain, the officer who would command his flagship.

But Collard had had no say at all in Dewar's selection. The Naval Secretary had written to him suggesting that he took Dewar, for it would be very difficult to substitute him. There was sound sense in the Naval Secretary's argument. Dewar was very senior in the list of captains and, if he were to gain promotion to flag rank himself, it was important that he accumulated the qualifying time of command at sea. Collard replied that he had no objection but added, with a typical touch, that he hoped the Naval Secretary would not tell Dewar that he had asked for him. He then received a letter from the First Lord of the Admiralty himself, notifying him that Dewar had got the appointment. It was not what the Navy's newest Rear-Admiral would have wished!

Captain Kenneth Gilbert Balmain Dewar was forty-eight years old and as tall as Collard was short. His straight, fair hair, now beginning to turn grey, was always meticulously parted down the centre in a line as straight as the set of his mouth.

The son of a prosperous Scottish doctor and educated in Edinburgh, Dewar was a thinker, what his fellow officers would call an 'X-chaser'. Like Collard, he had specialized in gunnery, but had gone further and later devoted himself to the study of naval strategy.

He was a quiet, haughty, somewhat withdrawn man. One admiral who knew him well said that Dewar came from the Kingdom of Fife 'where men are born getting out of bed on the wrong side and spend all their lives trying to get over it'. He usually made himself so unobtrusive that, even as captain, many of his ship's company were unaware that he was on board for days on end.

Yet for all his reticence he was capable of getting himself into extremely hot water. His notions on strategy were mainly to blame. Invited to read a paper before a gathering of senior officers at Staff College, he had delivered a highly critical lecture instead. He had argued that naval thinking was out of date. Nelson had evolved his battle tactics because his ships were ruled by the wind. That was no excuse for them being slavishly followed so many years afterwards. Senior officers dislike being criticized even by inference and Dewar was regarded by most of his audience as an impertinent young pup, but there were others, important names among them, who shared his views and supported him.

Such backing and his own ability had given him command of *Royal Oak*. He joined her on 6 November, exactly a week before Collard.

Commander Henry Martin Daniel, DSO, the third of the trio, was also a gunnery expert. He was just 39 years of age and joined *Royal Oak* on Christmas Eve, more than a month after Collard and Daniel, but while they had no recent experience of naval life in Malta, he was an old Mediterranean hand.

The commander's job aboard a warship, particularly a battleship and especially a flagship, is no sinecure. His whole career depends on the success he makes of it. The admiral himself is, in some respects, a passenger aboard his own flagship, albeit a most influential passenger, rather like the chairman of an airline who books a flight aboard one of his company's aircraft. Collard's primary concern was with the group of ships he commanded. It was Dewar's task to run the *Royal Oak*.

Like any other commander in his position, it was Daniel's duty to carry out his captain's wishes. More than that, to anticipate them and to inspire the whole ship's company to such a height of efficiency that Dewar could regard his ship contentedly and Collard look on his flagship with approval.

In the Royal Navy promotion to the rank of lieutenant-commander is by seniority, and after that, by selection. Daniel had cleared the first hurdle. He had been a commander for five and a half years when he joined *Royal Oak*. Whether he ever became a captain or not would depend very largely on what Collard and Dewar thought of him.

Tall, with fair, crinkled hair and ears pointed in rather elfin fashion, Daniel was a competent officer and cool in action; he had seen a great deal of that, having served practically the whole of the late war at sea. Besides being awarded the Distinguished Service Order, he had been mentioned in dispatches. He was also a specimen of some curiosity in a naval wardroom for, as a practising Christian Scientist, he openly prayed for his fellow officers and in a previous ship had actually held prayer meetings on the lower deck. This could hardly have gone down well with Dewar who was a firm Roman Catholic and, according to at least one colleague, a 'very superior person'. Daniel was a sanctimonious man and on occasion could be most temperamental. To add to all this, he was a frustrated playwright and impresario. The Navy was fond of its shipboard entertainment and its amateur dramatics and it never had a more ardent sketch-writer, stage manager and producer than Daniel.

The Navy also had a splendid reputation for entertaining the outside world. Wherever it sailed its hospitality was renowned, from formal and diplomatic occasions when foreign potentates were entertained, to summer cocktail parties when 'Showing the Flag' off some seaside holiday resort, not forgetting dances on board ship in any port the Fleet might be based. Then there were the children's parties when gun turrets would be spectacularly disguised as huge elephants and canvas chutes rigged to become exciting slides. In a place like Malta ships were judged by their sociability and hospitality as much as they were by their seagoing efficiency. And it was generally recognized that any vessel fortunate enough to have Daniel aboard to organize affairs was a very lucky ship indeed. His parties were spectacular. He once arranged a fancy dress dance with the opera *Die Fledermaus* as the theme and spent most of the night dressed as a spectacular bat clinging to the underside of the quarterdeck awnings over the dancers' heads.

Percy Barnacle was promoted Royal Marine Bandmaster, First Class, aboard *Royal Oak* on 14 November, 1928, at the age of 35, just one day after Collard joined her. Physically he and his Admiral were much alike, for Barnacle was just five feet, six inches tall and almost as stocky. There the similarity ended. Barnacle was a quiet, modest man, never heard to swear. He was a deeply devout Christian with a most unhappy background. His father George had served in the British Army Commissariat in Burma. He looked an imposing man, with moustaches, high-collared blue frockcoat, black-braided frogs across his chest and pillbox cap with its cheesecutter peak. Before he left Burma to come home and retire he had no trouble at all in persuading the young daughter of a fellow non-commissioned officer to marry him.

Poor girl. All she had known was Burma and a life where even NCOs had servants. London's climate was one of the least of her troubles as she learnt to shop, polish and keep house. In addition she had two small children, Percy and his younger sister.

George Barnacle eventually found himself a job as foreman with the Lea Valley Water Company. Then, one afternoon, when he was in his fifties and having tea in the kitchen with his family, he had a heart attack and dropped dead. Disaster followed tragedy. The house in which they lived belonged to the company and widow and children were ordered to quit. Destitute, they had nowhere to go, no one to whom they could turn. They even slept at night under street traders' barrows in London's back streets.

It is said that, in her desperation, the widow turned to prostitution. In any case she did not live long. When he was eight years old Percy Barnacle and his small sister found themselves inmates of an orphanage in Salford, Lancashire. Founded by Sir William Barnes, a well-known local philanthropist, it was an enlightened institution by the standards of the day. What is more, it had a band. Percy learnt to play the trombone so well that when he was almost sixteen years old he tried to join the Royal Marines as a bandboy. At first he was rejected as being over-age but when they heard him play an exception was made.

During the war he was serving in HMS *Britannia* when she was torpedoed. He was trapped in the gunnery control deep in the heart of the ship. It was an experience that stayed clear and sharp with him ever afterwards.

Percy Barnacle was a man who knew his place and never stepped out of it. So all the recent comings and goings aboard *Royal Oak*, the arrival of Collard, Dewar and Daniel, were no concern of his – or so he thought!

He was also a busy man. Apart from his routine duties he was trying to turn a group of volunteer sailors into a passable jazz band.

Like her four sister ships, *Royal Oak* was designed to serve as a flagship from time to time. There might have to be some shuffling of cabins to accommodate the Admiral's staff, but Collard's own quarters were spacious and splendid. His day cabin alone was as large as any liner's stateroom and considerably roomier than most. It was located in the stern, on the upper deck, immediately below the quarterdeck. It extended the full width of the ship and was very comfortably furnished with well-stuffed sofas and armchairs. Collard's roll-top writing desk, complete with bell-push to summon his staff, was over on the port side. On a warm day, with the ports open to create a breeze, and the sunny reflection of the water in Grand Harbour rippling on the impeccably white enamelled deckhead, it must have been a pleasant place from which to run affairs.

Through a doorway beside the fireplace and beyond the desk was the Admiral's dining cabin, occupied largely by a six-foot-long polished table. Beyond that cabin again was Collard's private pantry. His bathroom, sleeping and guest cabins were over on the starboard side. Opposite, and considerably smaller, was Dewar's suite of day and sleeping cabins. Extending forward were the quarters of the ship's most senior officers, until they reached two large compartments either side of the upper deck. These were the Royal Marine messes in their traditional place.

It has always been said, and not always jokingly, that the Marines are situated where they are in order to protect the officers from the ratings berthed at the other end of the ship.

Not that Collard had much opportunity to explore his new quarters, at least for a little while. Aided by tugs, *Royal Oak*, either alone or in company, put to sea nearly every day for training in readiness for the annual Combined Spring Exercises with the Atlantic Fleet, and Collard spent most of the time on his bridge just above the navigating platform where Dewar was running the ship.

Like so many other officers, Collard and Dewar had settled their wives in accommodation ashore and joined them every evening. In the early morning and late afternoon Grand Harbour became a nautical version of a city commuter rush hour with the white wakes of launches and barges criss-crossing the churning waters. Though, what with the wailing of bo's'ns' calls, there was considerably more ceremony than the mere salute of a doorman when the occupants arrived or departed.

From time to time Collard and Dewar did manage to eat together on board. These meals were rather odd affairs – the Admiral his bluff and hearty self, his Flag Captain reticent almost to the point of total silence.

Yet they were in harmony except, perhaps, for one small riffle. Apart from her outward smartness and her workaday efficiency, a ship was judged by her discipline and the blankness of her periodic 'crime' returns. *Royal Oak* had three stokers awaiting decision on a charge of assaulting

1 Admiral of the Fleet Sir Roger Keyes. "Determined to prove himself the greatest Keyes of them all". (p. 14).

2 Rear Admiral B.St.G. Collard. "He looked every short inch the part of a naval officer". (p.18) (*Leslie Gardiner*)

a petty officer, a very serious charge indeed. Collard was all for having them court-martialled forthwith. Dewar, on the other hand, had listened to the men's story, was inclined to suspect the petty officer's conduct and had asked for an investigation. Collard said no more about it.

They had both been aboard the ship for a month when Christmas came, with the usual children's party and high jinks. Having only joined *Royal Oak* on Christmas Eve, Commander Daniel was unable to exercise his flair for organizing such events, but his chance was to come soon. On Thursday, 12 January the officers were to have a dance. It was a very important event in *Royal Oak*'s social calendar. As a newly appointed flagship, it was her great opportunity to show the whole Mediterranean Fleet exactly how such an affair should be conducted. Pride and honour were deeply involved.

If Rear-Admiral Collard had one paramount fault it was his utter, total and unfailing inability to delegate authority. Even as a captain and later as an admiral it was rarely sufficient for him to give an order and stand back until it was reported to him that it had been carried out. He could not resist investigating for himself. He had even been known, with many a roar and bellow, to organize the seating for Sunday service aboard his ship. This habit not only amused the crew but also endeared him to them. It was not often they had the chance to watch a senior officer wearing an armful of gold braid personally supervising the placing of a capstan bar, while the junior officer or petty officer who was supposed to do the job stood by helplessly.

So, although it was none of his affair, it was far too much to expect Collard to have no say in the forthcoming dance. But perhaps it was his affair after all. For he had decided that, while *Royal Oak* was in all her festive glory, he would give his first real dinner party aboard that same night.

The most junior and most recently appointed flag officer was going to entertain his Commander-in-Chief, Sir Roger Keyes, and Lady Keyes, together with others among Malta's notables.

That bell on his desk rarely stopped ringing – and it was always Daniel he wished to see. Up until then their relationship had been brief and routine. Now Commander Daniel was the man of the hour. Collard demanded that what he called the 'whisky bar' in the wardroom be closed on the night of the dance. He was well aware that some of the older and more senior officers, particularly those whose wives were not

25

in Malta, regarded dancing as tiresome and would prefer to observe the gaiety on the quarterdeck with a cold eye and promptly go below to the wardroom, order a stiff drink and have a happy time criticizing what they had witnessed.

There would be none of that, for a start. What there would be were plenty of officers standing by as dancing partners. No wife, no sister, no daughter would be left in loneliness. Collard was adamant. There would be no wallflowers on board his ship!

Line after line of coloured lights were rigged; the sacrosanct quarter-deck, bleached almost white through endless scrubbing, found itself treated to a generous dose of French chalk; flowers and greenery by the armful were ordered, a long bar was set up, carpet was laid and under *Royal Oak*'s aftermost pair of fifteen-inch guns that shadowed the quarterdeck – gleaming painted barrels, their muzzles plugged by gilt and white tampions bearing the motif of a Stuart crown surrounded by oakleaves – a platform for the dance band was rigged. The arrangement was that the Royal Marine band should play waltzes, foxtrots and suchlike for two-thirds of the night and that the newly trained volunteer naval jazz band would perform in between, while the Marines had a break, something to eat and, with any luck, a drink or two.

The weather that January Thursday in Malta had not distinguished itself. There had been little sunshine but the evening was mild and windless, and even to the most sophisticated partygoer among the guests assembling at Custom House Steps in Valletta there was something quite exceptional about an evening aboard a great battleship – the burble of the idling launches as they took their turn to embark their invited cargo, the attentiveness of the young midshipmen commanding them, the impeccable boathook drill of the seamen at bow and stern, then the trip across the harbour to the *Royal Oak*, looming ghostly grey under the night sky, in her pale Mediterranean paintwork with her quarterdeck brilliantly bright and the strains of Bandmaster Barnacle's band drifting over the water.

The launches arrived alongside the accommodation ladders; there were arc lamps to light the way; helping hands were waiting; so were the messmen in their spotless white jackets, holding out silver trays of well-filled glasses. At the sight of all this even those naval wives who had attended so many shipboard dances – even these who only a couple of hours before had listened to their husbands cursing as they forced reluctant studs into unyieldingly stiff dress-shirt fronts – felt that *Royal Oak* was putting on quite a show.

26

One deck below, in the Admiral's dining cabin, things had gone just as well. The Commander-in-Chief, Sir Roger Keyes, was always an easy guest. So was his wife. The food was good, drink was plentiful and the conversation robust and cheery, exactly the sort that Keyes and Collard appreciated.

His first venture in entertainment at such a level over, Collard saw his guests ashore. He must have been a satisfied man as he decided to visit the quarterdeck and attend the dance. If so, his satisfaction did not last for long!

4

'Call Yourself a Bandmaster?'

WHAT COLLARD SAW when he went on to the quarterdeck displeased him greatly – there were guests without dancing partners. This might have been understandable as it was the first dance of the night but it made no difference to the Admiral. He headed straight for Captain Dewar.

Now Dewar and his Commander had taken special steps to ensure that a proportion of officers took turns to refrain from dancing with their own personal guests. Instead, they were to spend the time effecting introductions. A roster had been made out and on it Dewar had restricted himself to only three dances and he was doing his duty as a host when Collard hurried over to him and, quite out of the blue and with no preamble at all, demanded, 'You are to make the Commander introduce people. You are to bite him. If you don't send for him and bite him, I will.'

Dewar was prompt enough to point out that Daniel was already dancing with a complete stranger, but he was so astonished by such an unexpected attack that he hardly knew what to say next. Moreover Collard was using his 'Hail the crow's nest' voice and a captain does not expect to be addressed like that on his own quarterdeck, particularly in front of guests. Collard saw his hesitation and snapped, 'If you don't I will make you rue it'.

He thundered off, this time with another bone to pick. If he had not liked what he had seen, then he most certainly did not like what he was hearing. He was standing by the bandstand when that dance ended and, as Daniel passed with his partner, he stopped him and said he wished to have words. The Commander could see by the Admiral's expression that all was very far from well, so he took his guest to a chair by the side of the quarterdeck and hurried back to Collard who promptly ordered him to dismiss the Royal Marine band and replace it with the volunteer sailors' jazz group.

Pointing to Barnacle and his men he stormed, 'I never heard such an awful row in my life. Everyone is complaining of it.' Daniel tried to explain that the programme had already been arranged between the two bands but the Admiral would have none of his excuses.

'If you cannot tell them, I will tell them myself. Come with me.'

Poor Dewar. Not only had he been shouted at on his own quarterdeck but now Collard was ordering his Commander about without having the grace to consult him first!

The Admiral and Daniel took the few paces to the front of the band-stand and stopped. Collard pointed his finger, beckoning for Barnacle to approach. Marines are rarely summoned by Admirals and Barnacle hastily obeyed. As he stood sharply to attention, Collard bawled at him, 'You call yourself a bandmaster? You are not fit to be in any ship, let alone a flagship. I have never heard such a bloody noise in my life.'

Royal Oak's quarterdeck was broad and long, and, with all the chatter of the officers and their guests, most of those further away in the stern of the ship, waiting for the band to start playing again, were unaware of what was going on. But not those near at hand. The surrounding officers and their dancing partners hastily withdrew, startled and embarrassed. It was for all the world like a host and hostess having a blazing row during a formal dinner party.

According to Daniel, the Admiral then lowered his voice to a more conversational level and he hoped the storm was over. But Collard said, 'Commander, that bandmaster is to go home tomorrow. I will not have him in the ship.'

The storm was not blown out yet. Raising his voice again and still only a yard or so away from the band, Collard exclaimed, 'I won't have a bugger like that in my ship.'

Nobody ever knew for certain how many guests heard the Admiral's explosion. Most of them were far too polite to comment, at least until they were back ashore. But, to put it mildly, his voice was robust and would have carried a fair way even if the music had not stopped.

Bandmaster Percy Barnacle was more than dumbfounded, he was shat-tered. All his life he had been an instinctive subscriber to the doctrine:

'God bless the Squire and his relations
And keep us in our proper stations.'

29

Even in later civilian life he persisted in calling his family doctor 'Sir'.

As far as he was concerned, an admiral was an admiral and a Royal Marine bandmaster a humble underling by comparison. But both had their proper roles to play and were to be respected in their performance. To be abused in such a way was more than he could comprehend.

Commander Daniel decided to take charge. He said to Barnacle, 'You are to play the next dance and I have given orders that the jazz band is to come aft and relieve you.' He then sought out the First Lieutenant and told him to round up the sailor members of the amateur band. Things did not go as smoothly as he hoped. Even in so brief a time a report of the Admiral's behaviour had reached the lower deck. The jazz band were in two minds whether they would perform at all – and as they were volunteers no one could order them to play.

The First Lieutenant sent for Daniel who finally persuaded them. Even so he had to take care that the dismissed Marine band and the sailors did not meet on the way to the quarterdeck. A muttered word or two and *Royal Oak*'s dance could have collapsed in scandal and disaster.

Instead it ended most successfully, spiced as it was with a touch of high drama. But at the end of the evening, as the anxious and indignant Dewar, tall and elegant in his black bow tie, stiff shirt and mess dress, was seeing his guests over the side, Collard approached him again. His voice had lost none of its bellow and, according to Dewar, his manner was excited. Again he was demanding that Percy Barnacle be sent home the next day, that the band playing had been disgraceful and that he would not have him in his flagship. Dewar did his best to shield his parting visitors from another scene by edging away from the turbulent Admiral. Yet, for the sake of his position, he had to protect his crew and, before he extricated himself, he insisted that the band was above average and pointed out how much trouble Barnacle had taken in training the sailors' jazz band – all voluntary work for the ship.

But Collard simply raised his voice even louder. 'You can have him in *your* ship. I won't have him in mine.'

Sparing the ears of the parting guests, Dewar moved away into the shadows.

Party over and quarterdeck deserted, the wardroom bar was open once again and *Royal Oak*'s officers spent an intriguing hour or two holding an inquest. In the Royal Marine's mess the talk was uglier. Among his sympathetic fellow senior non-commissioned officers, Percy Barnacle was beginning to calm down, though his sense of outrage was increased by the hurt of being called a bugger. It was not the word itself. Although Barnacle never swore and was deeply religious, he had been at sea far too long to take offence at a careless swear word. It was the fact that an admiral had used it and used it in such a situation. Barnacle made up his mind. He would resign from the Royal Marines the next morning.

If only Rear-Admiral Collard had approached the Bandmaster in a gentler fashion and asked him, as man to man, what he thought of the band's performance, things might have been very different. For privately Percy Barnacle had great contempt for the musicians the Royal Marines had provided and called them a 'Squeegy' band, which, for a non-swearer, was pretty strong stuff. Also, his clarinettist was an alcoholic who managed to lay his hands on far more of the crew's daily rum ration than was good for him.

Friday the Thirteenth, the following morning, did not start at all well aboard *Royal Oak*. The approaches to the Admiral's day cabin on the upper deck, and the cabin flat leading to it, lost much of their monastic calm. Normally a tranquil haven of glittering brass and spotless paintwork surveyed by a contemplative sentry in white cap cover and pipeclayed belt, now there was a certain commotion about the place.

First, the Church of England Chaplain, the Reverend Harry Goulding, demanded an audience of the Admiral and Collard agreed to see him. Unlike the other services, naval chaplains, although they wear officers' uniforms, have cabins and mess in the wardroom, have no badges of rank. This can be a considerable disadvantage when facing the gold braid of a full blown rear-admiral. But now Collard had caught a tiger by the tail. Goulding was no whey-faced curate but a man who had served as a seaman on the lower deck during the late war and was not given to blushing nor stammering.

Bandmaster Barnacle had seen him earlier in what the Chaplain described as great agony of mind and had told him that he wished to leave the ship, to resign from the Royal Marines even if it meant foregoing his pension. What was more, a number of the bandsmen wanted to quit *Royal Oak* forthwith.

'I wish to see you,' said Goulding to his Admiral. 'I have heard you called the bandmaster a bugger.'

Collard instantly and hotly denied this. He demanded to know who had told the Chaplain this, but Goulding refused to say.

Stormily, Collard gave his personal word of honour that Goulding

31

could contradict the story whenever he heard it mentioned. Almost immediately afterwards the startled Chaplain thought that the Admiral was about to attack him as the furious Collard rose from his roll-top desk and raised his arm. In fact he was seeking his bellpush. He wanted Dewar – and rapidly.

The moment Dewar entered the day cabin, his cap with its gilded peak under his arm, Collard exploded and told him what the Chaplain had said. Dewar promptly answered that he had used the word 'bugger', adding, 'The Commander told me you did.'

The Admiral reached for his bellpush again. Within minutes Commander Daniel had joined them.

Collard's first words were, 'Commander, the Chaplain has been aft here and told me that I called the bandmaster a bugger. Now you were there and can bear me out that I did nothing of the sort, did I?'

Picking his words with all the care of an old lady walking down an icebound garden path, Daniel replied, 'If you ask me whether you called him a bugger I say "No", but if you ask me whether you referred to him as a bugger in the presence of the band, I say "Yes".'

This fine distinction did nothing to soothe the Admiral. He swore on his honour that he had never used the word. What is more, it was not in his vocabulary. By now he was in a furious temper and shouted something about it all ending in a court martial, but whose court martial he did not define. However, Daniel persisted. He told Collard that nothing would make him budge from a statement that he knew to be correct.

Later, another storm blew up. Major Claude Attwood, Commanding Officer of *Royal Oak*'s Royal Marine detachment, arrived on board from a gunnery exercise ashore. Attwood had been at the dance and, when he heard the commotion, had made to interfere. Very wisely, his dancing partner had held him back. Now he demanded to see the Captain to protest at the slur on his unit, which included the band. But Dewar was as elusive and as self-effacing as ever. He delegated the Commander to deal with the protest.

Dewar was being logical. The molehill was well on its way to becoming a mountain already. The lower the level at which any protest was made the better.

Attwood did not even try to disguise his indignation from Daniel. He made an angry protest at what he regarded as a reflection on his Corps and himself. He was also inspired by a feeling that if he did not react strongly then, he would have trouble maintaining discipline in his detachment. He felt there might be trouble if he did not act at once. As it was, the band was already discouraged and outraged.

Having made his case, the Royal Marine Major told Dewar that he left the matter entirely in the Captain's hands. He also hinted that if the Captain wanted to take matters further, then he was quite ready to help.

This conversation with Daniel was interrupted by a message to join the Captain in Collard's day cabin, for a second and much longer discussion with the Admiral. This time a plan was evolved. Daniel was to have an entirely free hand to interview Bandmaster Barnacle. He was to cross-examine him closely to find out if he actually heard the Admiral swear at him and then he was to find out exactly what were Barnacle's views of the situation. In short, a peace-making expedition.

Daniel sent for Barnacle, asked him to sit down and set about his plan. It became very plain that the Bandmaster knew he had been sworn at. What is more, he provided the names of five other bandsmen who had also heard. Then Daniel said, 'The Admiral has made a very generous *amende* which he has asked me to convey to you. I feel certain you will appreciate it.'

'Thank you very much,' said Percy Barnacle who had obviously grasped the meaning of such diplomatic niceties. He rose from his seat, saluted and walked away. After all, it is not every day that one gets an apology, even a devious one, from an admiral. And that was the last to be heard of his threat to resign from the Service.

The strange thing that escaped all the officers – Admiral, Flag Captain, Commander and Major – was that Barnacle could not have resigned even if he had wished to. Such a privilege was not open to non-commissioned officers.

Daniel later claimed that Collard congratulated him afterwards. He also added that the Admiral thanked him for getting out of a damned nasty hole. This Collard heatedly denied.

Major Attwood was not so easy to pacify. On the following Sunday morning Daniel had a quiet word with him on the quarterdeck. He said that the Admiral had apologized and made redress that was satisfactory to the Captain and asked Attwood if he, too, was prepared to accept. Attwood said he would, but added darkly that, should any further incident take place, then he reserved the right to refer again to this one.

That conversation was not the only effort at peace-making on the Sabbath. Collard came offshore in his barge with a party of ladies, including his wife. They were going to attend church service. By that time practically the whole ship's company was assembled aft. Daniel made a point of sitting next to the Admiral, while the congregation watched warily and closely. He even told Collard a joke to show on what good terms they were.

After the service Daniel went to his cabin and wrote a note to Collard, which was speedily delivered. It read: 'We should esteem it a great honour if you will come to the wardroom for a cocktail but I realize you have ladies on board and if you cannot get away we shall fully understand.'

(By custom and tradition, the Admiral and his Flag Captain are never members of the flagship's wardroom mess but attend only as invited guests.)

The Admiral came and Daniel rounded up every officer who was available, including Major Attwood. The gathering was cordial. Collard even stayed for a second cocktail.

After he left, Daniel addressed all the officers in the anteroom. He told them that what had just occurred was the Western version of what the Orientals called taking their salt. The Admiral had eaten their salt. Now the incident of the dance was to be absolutely closed.

So it was. No more mention was made of it – with one exception. Not long afterwards Daniel was in the wardroom with Attwood and another officer. The Major harked back to the dance.

Daniel frowned and left them. A few moments later he sent for Attwood to join him on the quarterdeck. Very formally he cautioned the Royal Marine and sent him about his business.

But for a long while afterwards, as one naval wife who knew Collard wrote, 'Bandmasters at ships' dances were inclined to be sensitive, and Admirals were selfconscious about addressing them.'

Alas for Daniel. He had not long to wait to discover how fragile was his newly-found cordiality with the Admiral. Finding his thespian talents cramped aboard *Royal Oak*, he had become involved with the local dramatic society. As soon as Collard learnt of this he grumbled to his Flag Captain that, as Daniel had such a reputation as an entertainments organizer, then he ought to employ his skills for the good of the ship and the Service and not waste his time ashore.

5

'Worse than a Bloody Midshipman'

T HROUGHOUT THE WEEK in which that remarkable dance took place Dewar
had been ashore each afternoon playing his part in a tactical exercise with
model ships on a tabletop ocean. He had been demonstrating to an audience
of junior officers his pet theory that British naval battle tactics had not
changed since the days of Nelson, the argument that had earned him such
a mixed reception when he had had the temerity to lecture his seniors on
a staff course some years before. During the week he had been deploying
his wooden fleet against an opponent behaving in textbook fashion. By
Friday evening the outcome was still undecided, which is hardly surprising
considering each player knew the other's hand. Collard presided as umpire
and arbiter.

On the Saturday, less than forty-eight hours after the dance, the war-
game party reassembled for the adjudication by Collard. There was a
large audience, headed by Keyes himself, with his second-in-command,
Joe Kelly. When it came to tactics Collard was a confirmed traditionalist.
Moreover, his Flag Captain's theories were a severe and implicit criticism
of the First Sea Lord, Earl Beatty, and his tactics at the Battle of Jutland,
a matter which had caused much controversy at the time and was still
being argued about by historians and in naval wardrooms.

Collard raised that booming voice of his and tore into Dewar and
all his theories. There was no malice in what he said, simply plain
scorn. As far as he was concerned his Flag Captain had wasted a lot
of valuable time demonstrating an idea that had been disproved over and
over again. But Dewar was not to be put down so easily. Dour, aesthetic

35

and intellectually autocratic, he argued back. His Admiral retorted by closing the exercise.

It was a highly entertaining time for the audience, especially for the junior officers. Keyes was not so amused. He was a little perturbed to see one of his Rear-Admirals and a flag captain arguing so hotly, particularly when they had been sharing the same ship for so short a time. He took Joe Kelly to one side and asked him to investigate the state of affairs aboard *Royal Oak*. News of the goings on at the Thursday night dance and its repercussions had clearly not reached Admiralty House. Or if it had, only by the back stairs.

So a couple of days later Vice-Admiral Kelly asked Collard to come and see him aboard *Warspite*. They had a quiet and private talk. Was there any friction between Collard and Dewar? Was Collard certain? The previous Saturday had displayed some tension. Collard denied that anything was wrong. He even praised his Flag Captain.

It has been said that by tradition and training Collard was the sort of man who could give no other answer. This might very well be true. Yet at the same time he must have been heavily aware that his behaviour at the dance a few nights before had put him at a sizeable disadvantage with Dewar. But Kelly was satisfied and Collard boarded his barge and returned to *Royal Oak* to dwell in coolly efficient and distant relationship with his Flag Captain.

The time for the Combined Spring Exercises, with the Atlantic Fleet sailing out from home waters, was approaching fast and *Royal Oak* spent long days at sea in endless drill. Matters were not helped by the Mediterranean weather which for the most part of early 1928 was unseasonably wet, sunless and rough, nor by a faulty port capstan engine that was giving *Royal Oak* and her forecastle officers considerable trouble.

On 5 March, a typically moody day, the ship was returning to her anchorage from exercise. It had been planned that she would reach home in darkness at about eleven p.m. Collard was due to sit in judgement at a court martial ashore the next day, so he ordered his Flag Lieutenant, Burghard, to make sure that his barge, which was lying alongside HMS *Valiant* in harbour, would come out and pick him up on time. It was the custom for a flag officer to leave his barge inshore while the flagship was on brief exercise, for the effort of swinging such a heavy launch inboard and outboard was labour-consuming and time-wasting, although only a day or so before Collard had told Dewar that in future he wished *Royal Oak* to put to sea with her full complement of boats on every occasion.

Burghard, who was no novice as an admiral's aide but a senior lieutenant about to be promoted, made sure that *Valiant* received the signal. Collard then instructed him in his usual fine detail to tell Commander Daniel that he wanted gangways on both sides of the quarterdeck prepared and ready for lowering with lights and boat ropes as he would be disembarking immediately the ship anchored. In case the weather was too rough a Jacob's ladder and extra deck lighting were to be ready.

Meanwhile in Collard's quarters his servant was carefully packing the full dress uniform that his master would need for the court martial: the frock coat, the epaulettes, the gold braid, the decorations, the highly polished shoes, starched linen, the stout leather case holding sword and gilt and black scabbard.

Because of the weather the exercise was cut short and it soon became clear that *Royal Oak* was going to return early. Collard sent Burghard to discover the new arrival time. The navigating bridge told him 'about 2045 hours'. So a new signal was made to the barge by way of *Valiant*. As the weather was freshening and the flagship was facing waves six to eight feet high with breakers all around, Collard decided that *Royal Oak* should anchor outside the breakwater for the night instead of attempting the channel into harbour.

At exactly the predicted time *Royal Oak* approached her anchorage, wind astern. Five minutes later Flag Lieutenant Burghard went down to the Admiral's day cabin and reported that the barge had put off from *Valiant*. Three minutes later he was back to say, 'The barge is coming up alongside the port side. The ship is stopped and the anchor's gone.'

Burghard was either over-optimistic or had been misinformed. On the rolling, pitching, torch-lit fo'c'sle there was trouble. The port capstan engine was up to its old tricks and the anchor cable had jammed.

All the same, at 2100 hours Collard appeared on the quarterdeck. He found little prepared. The gangway had not been lowered, the boat rope was not rigged. If the weather was inclined to be stormy, the Admiral's temper was considerably worse. There he stood with his Flag Lieutenant beside him and his luggage-laden servant near at hand and no one except a baffled officer of the watch to attend him. On such a night and such an occasion he did not expect the full ceremony due to an admiral leaving his flagship but at least his flag captain should have been in attendance and the commander there to supervise his departure. On that dark, cloudy night lit only by the swaying decklights, there was no sign of either. It was all due to a simple misunderstanding – or two, or three.

37

The weather was not so very bad. Just sufficient to make the crew of *Royal Oak* realize that they were sailors and to set carelessly stowed gear tumbling and rolling across a mess deck. But handling a great battleship of 29,000 tons at dead-slow speed was never easy, particularly anchoring with a following wind. Even if the port capstan engine had been behaving itself, it was unthinkable that any Royal Navy captain would delegate the duty to even the most competent subordinate, certainly not a captain as senior as Dewar, soon due to become a rear-admiral himself.

He was fully occupied on the navigating bridge and not in the least concerned about Collard who that morning had expressed himself satisfied to leave the ship at eleven p.m. Now, thanks to circumstances, he was over two hours early. So Captain Dewar, content that the Admiral had plenty of time to disembark at leisure, concentrated on securing his ship. He was utterly unaware that Collard had been following his service-long habit of taking things into his own hands and making personal arrangements for boarding his barge at the earliest possible moment.

Dewar was busy. It was important that he got a good swing on the ship by using his engines to bring *Royal Oak* rapidly into the wind before he let the anchor cables run out. Normally Commander Daniel would have been at hand to attend to the Admiral but he had his mind on that misbehaving port capstan engine and quite rightly decided his duty was on the fo'c'sle. It was just as well he was there, for the port anchor cable had jammed. If it could not be freed, then the ship would have to ride to her starboard anchor only. It was a moment for experience and watchful orders. The Admiral could wait. For Daniel, like Dewar, had assumed that with *Royal Oak*'s early arrival the Admiral would take his time in leaving after the ship had finally swung to anchor and the wind and sea had dictated which would be the wiser gangway to lower.

Collard, obsessed with his own departure, had very different ideas. He was not going to wait for *Royal Oak* to settle at her anchorage. Angrily he despatched his Flag Lieutenant to bring Dewar to the port gangway and ordered a young and awed junior officer to find Daniel. The Commander arrived first. In fact, with the recalcitrant port cable cleared, he was already on his way when he got the message. Furiously Collard ordered him to lower the gangway. For the first time Daniel understood that the Admiral was determined to leave the ship even while she was still swinging. The operation took some minutes, with the barge, which had faced a rough passage, plunging and tossing, now and again completely out of sight, off *Royal Oak*'s port quarter. Yet Collard was a fine seaman of the old school and had rightly calculated that in a few moments the port side would be sheltered from the wind and that embarking aboard the launch would be simple. During the delay Dewar arrived. He had left the bridge reluctantly for his ship was still not at rest.

Royal Oak's heaving quarterdeck was wide but that night it was unusually well populated. Apart from the Officer of the Watch and his acolytes and the hands rigging the gangway, there was a section of Royal Marines doing exercise and a party of seamen under punishment being found work for reluctant hands to do. Most of them were to have a happy time listening to authority falling out. For as Collard's voice matched his fury, many a windborne word came their way. Dewar, for his part, had the benefit of every harsh word. Collard stormed that he could not get a single order obeyed in the bloody ship – no ladder, no nothing. He shouted that he was treated worse than a midshipman, that he would not stay in the rotten ship and would ask to have his flag shifted.

Dewar, in his turn, demanded that the Admiral tell him of a single occasion when his orders had not been carried out, and then, more quietly and in an effort to bring some decorum into the proceedings, said that he would inquire into the reason why the port ladder was not ready.

It was then that Collard growled a remark that was to put the careers of all three men in jeopardy:

'I should damned well think so and get the Commander's reasons in writing.'

Within fifteen minutes of *Royal Oak* dropping her anchors – the port capstan engine had finally been persuaded to make itself useful – Collard's barge was lifting and rolling through the breaking seas, shorebound, complete with servant and luggage. Dewar hurried back to the bridge. The anchor cables were still being veered. It was another eight minutes or so before he could give the order 'Finish with main engines. Secure cables'.

Daniel went down to the wardroom for a well-earned drink. A group of officers was talking and he heard the words: 'Another bust-up on the quarterdeck'. The mercurial Commander obviously decided to regard the entire episode as a joke, for he just laughed and said, 'I haven't been called anything I haven't been called before,' then ordered a whisky and soda for himself and a couple of other officers. He did not know then what high words had passed between the Admiral and the Flag Captain.

It was some time afterwards that Daniel visited the Captain's cabin and was told that he had to submit an explanation in writing to the Admiral, to account for the confusion on the quarterdeck.

A demand for an 'Explanation in writing' from a senior officer could have two distinct effects. A simple, lucid and justifiable account of an incident might well settle the matter there and then and for all time. On the other hand, if not acceptable, it could be a significant smear on the record of an officer like Daniel whose next promotion, to captain, would be entirely by selection and in a highly competitive field at that.

Had Collard, whose volcanic temper was spectacular but usually short lived, received such an explanation a day or so later the betting is a boathook to a battleship that he would normally have dismissed it with no more than a mild wonder at all the fuss. Unhappily for the Rear-Admiral, the Flag Captain and the Commander, *Royal Oak* was about to try her hand at slap-stick comedy.

The court martial over, Collard signalled that he would be returning to the ship at 1745 hours. Stung by the Admiral's bellow the day before that he could not get a single thing done as he wished, Dewar made absolutely certain that Collard would not find the most minute flaw in his flagship on his return. The gangway was lowered – this time it was obvious which was the sheltered side of the ship – the ceremonial side party was mustered, a signalman stood ready to hoist Collard's flag, for, like a monarch, an admiral's ensign is not flown in his absence. Daniel, telescope underarm, prowled the ship like an anxious housekeeper.

The only possibly unhappy soul aboard was Lieutenant-Commander Archie Alastair Stewart Murray. He was the second senior lieutenant-commander in *Royal Oak* and Daniel's shadow. Mindful of Collard's instruction of only a couple of days before that the ship would always carry her full complement of boats whenever she put to sea, Daniel had delegated him to supervise the swinging inboard of the Admiral's barge by means of a derrick.

The sea and the wind had hardly abated since the day before, the waves were still quite high, there was plenty of broken water around and *Royal Oak*, for all her size, was rolling in matronly fashion. Yet it was not an impracticable exercise. Murray would have cheerfully embarked any ship's launch except an admiral's barge, and Collard's barge at that. Weighing nearly four tons, the idea of all that immaculate paintwork, that cherished varnish, those gilded brass dolphins – one sudden lurch of the ship, one unforgiving steel stay in the way. It was not a thing to dwell on. Murray studied the assembled ratings patiently waiting to haul the barge inboard and wished he had some other task to do that darkening evening.

40

Under the heavy sky Collard's barge was seen butting its way through the crested waves towards the ship. The ceremonial side party had assembled at the head of the gangway. Dewar, Daniel, the Duty Lieutenant-Commander and the Officer of the Watch gathered some paces inboard ready to receive their Admiral with all the ceremony that had been so lacking when he had left the ship. The quarterdeck of *Royal Oak* was so broad that from where they were standing the barge would soon disappear under the lee of the ship's side and the first they would see of Collard would be when he mounted the gangway and his head drew level with the edge of *Royal Oak*'s deck. But the Admiral never appeared at all!

It was clear that no dire disaster had befallen him – he had not tumbled and fallen into the sea – for his familiar roar could be heard above the wind. Then, before the startled eyes of the waiting officers, the side party standing stiffly at attention by the side of the ship suddenly disappeared down the gangway, led by the corporal of the guard and the side boys.

What had happened was that when the barge drew alongside the rising and falling lower gangway grating, one moment swilling with water, the next a foot or two out of it, Collard, the prime seaman, had waited his moment and, despite his limp, had nipped on to it with his shoes bone dry. He had been half-way up the accommodation ladder before he heard and felt the sudden surge of a rogue wave. Looking down over his shoulder, he saw his servant burdened with luggage, regalia and sword case, awash on the lower grating. Undoubtedly Collard's first thought was that some hundreds of pound's worth of valuable and totally uninsured kit was about to be swept away. His second, and just as certain, was why the hell there was no handling party waiting to assist his man.

He raised a furious voice and had the once formally arranged side party scrambling down the ladder past him.

On the quarterdeck, with all this pandemonium out of sight, all was formally aligned, patient and calm. Collard was no doubt having one of his tantrums. He had discovered some small fault on his way up the gangway and, as usual forgetting that he was an admiral, had taken matters into his own hands. No officer even bothered to step to the side of the ship and look down.

It was simply one more misunderstanding.

That there were no seamen waiting to help Collard's servant with his luggage was simply on account of the Admiral's direction of a couple of days earlier, namely that *Royal Oak* should embark all boats before sailing, including his own barge. The obvious way to deal with his luggage was to leave it in the barge until it had been swung inboard and unload it then. But either Collard had forgotten his order or, weatherwise as he was, thought, like Lieutenant-Commander Murray, that hoisting the barge inboard was not worth the risk. Whatever the reason he had not discussed it with his officers.

When Collard finally reached the quarterdeck he was in a towering fury. Pausing only to lean over the side and bellow to the coxswain of the barge to return to HMS *Valiant*, he headed for his quarters with his Flag Lieutenant at his heels. On the way he passed the rank of saluting officers without so much as a bob of his head. In front of a very fair number of *Royal Oak*'s ship's company he cut her Captain dead!

This was an insult both to the ship and himself that Dewar could never forgive. From that moment on and as long as they were in the ship the Flag Captain never spoke another direct word to the Admiral – save, perhaps, once. It was always the custom for Admiral and Flag Captain to share a midday meal together in the Admiral's quarters. Dewar elected to have luncheon alone in his own cabin but Collard, who was as ready to make amends as he was to lose his temper, did once invite him to share his table. Dewar attended but the evidence is that he sat and ate in total and uncomfortable silence. He was a proud Scotsman and he had been insulted once too often.

It was a ridiculous situation – two senior officers who had been together barely twelve weeks now so utterly divided. As stupid as the reasons. And what were they? A few hot words at a dance; a ship's boat delayed for a few moments; a confusion over some luggage.

It was even more absurd than that. Collard's appointment to *Royal Oak* was for only a year. Not a long time, some would say, for two utterly incompatible but highly experienced officers to broaden their shoulders and smother their feelings.

But two days later, on 8 March, even Collard threw away his olive branch. On that day the flagship was at sea again, this time in company with her sister battleships *Ramillies* and *Resolution*. The original orders were that on their return to harbour from exercise *Royal Oak* was to take Number 12 berth and *Ramillies* Number 13, but early in the day, and for reasons known only to that bureaucratic establishment ashore that Keyes had allowed to flourish, the berthing orders were reversed. *Royal Oak* was to use Number 13. *Ramillies* was to make for Number 12.

At the end of a long day at sea and getting on for midnight, all three battleships were approaching harbour. Collard was up in his lair keeping

42

a watchful eye on his small fleet, Dewar on the bridge below, handling *Royal Oak*. Although buoy 12 was the innermost berth and consequently *Ramillies* should have led the way into harbour, Collard ordered *Royal Oak* to enter first.

It is important to remember that Collard had not chosen Dewar as his flag captain. The man of his picking would undoubtedly have been someone of his own nature, extrovert and hearty – a thoroughgoing bluff seaman. The sort of captain who in such a situation would have said to himself, 'I bet the old man's not spotted the change of berthing orders,' and have cheerily, but respectfully, attracted his admiral's attention. Not so Dewar. He had read the orders, and he knew it was Collard's duty to read and sign the signal log in which they were contained.

At 11.30 that night the flagship edged slowly into harbour – and headed straight for Number 13 berth! The dumbfounded Collard turned on his Flag Lieutenant and demanded that he find out why. But Burghard already knew. He informed his master that the Rear-Admiral Malta had amended the orders early that morning and, like Dewar, had assumed that Collard had read the signal log before he signed it.

On the bridge below, Dewar had already decided that his Admiral's order for the flagship to enter first was wrong. However, he reckoned that *Ramillies* was a good half-hour's steaming astern and that, with the help of harbour tugs, *Royal Oak* would be safely moored and out of the way by the time her sister ship arrived. Even so, he did not envy *Ramillies*' captain the task of handling his ship through the narrow strip of water between *Royal Oak* and the massive aircraft carrier *Eagle* lying opposite.

As it happened things went appallingly wrong. Both tugs towing the flagship parted their hawsers and the helpless *Royal Oak* swung right across the harbour, blocking the entrance. Dewar had to send for the Flag Lieutenant and tell him, 'You had better ask the Admiral to make a signal to *Ramillies* to keep clear while our stern is coming round.'

Finally the ships were safely berthed. Fortunately it had happened so late at night that there were few expert sightseers to observe such goings-on. Even so there were more than enough for Collard. This time he did not fly into a fury, for he appreciated that the fault was his and his alone. Instead he became unusually and dangerously quiet – and completely unforgiving. He had found Dewar a difficult man to handle in the past, but that was endurable. Now the man had turned out to be utterly disloyal and untrustworthy. Dewar was not only *Royal Oak*'s Captain but also his own personal Flag Captain, a man who should be a confidante and a stout support. By not reminding him of the change of berthing orders Dewar had proved himself totally unreliable. Most of his fellow flag officers would probably have agreed with him. Dewar, on the other hand, merely said that the idea of telling Collard about the new arrangements never entered his head.

Neither officer realized how little more time they would have to endure each other's company.

Commander Daniel had no direct part to play in this last episode, except that, as executive officer, any slur on *Royal Oak*'s reputation for efficiency reflected on him. However, he had other things on his mind. Three nights before, he had settled down to his Admiral's demand for a written explanation of the confusion over the gangways. He took the matter very seriously. First of all he sought out every officer remotely concerned, to find out if anything had gone wrong. Was there anything at all to justify the Admiral's complaint? Finding nothing, he retreated to his cabin and started to write. He wrote for a long time, for it was a long letter, phrased in the official parlance that years in the Royal Navy had taught him. Each paragraph was neatly numbered and there were eleven paragraphs in all.

It was a letter that was to destroy two careers!

The first paragraph was merely preamble. The rest read as follows:–

'2. In the first dog watch the Flag Lieutenant reported that the Rear-Admiral required to leave the ship on our return to the anchorage and that he was arranging for the barge to meet the ship. He also delivered a message from the Rear-Admiral that he required me to have a boat rope, yardarm group (a lighting cluster) and Jacob's ladder ready in case it was too rough to use the accommodation ladder, as he did not wish any risk incurred of the barge being broken up. The interpretation which I placed on this message was that the immunity of the barge from damage was the primary consideration. I gave the necessary orders for the provision of the gear and for the requisite hands, adding orders for the provision of extra fenders, heaving lines, etc.

'3. The gunnery programme was altered and in consequence the time of anchoring was suddenly advanced two hours. This information was received at 1930 and I immediately sent the hands to supper.

'4. I made inquiries from the fore bridge whether there would be any choice of sides for the Rear-Admiral's disembarkation and was informed in the negative; that the ship would be letting go the anchor at 2045, stern to wind. The ship would presumably swing head to wind and accordingly (there being no choice of sides) I ordered that the starboard accommodation ladder should be prepared for instant lowering, but it was not to be lowered without my orders. This restriction was imposed because in my judgement it seemed likely to be too rough for the barge to come alongside the accommodation ladder, and in any case I anticipated plenty of time whilst the ship was swinging to her cable. I made it clear that the starboard accommodation ladder must be completely ready, and that the Jacob's ladder, boat rope, etc. were also to be ready either side. If any hitch occurred I expected to be informed by the Officer in Charge, Lieutenant Lionel H. Phillips and I personally went forward to make arrangement for the freeing of the port cable holder which had jammed the capstan engine. For this purpose I used the remainder of the starboard watch and stayed forward in case of any mishap with the other bower anchor. As soon as any possibility of any such mishap had passed I turned to go aft, and whilst cable was still being paid out I received a message that the Rear-Admiral wished to see me. I went aft forthwith and on arrival on the quarterdeck found a great commotion at the port ladder. Lieutenant Phillips informed me that the Rear-Admiral had ordered the barge alongside the port side and that he was angry because the port accommodation ladder was not down. I told him to proceed with all despatch and reported myself to the Rear-Admiral. As ratings were close at hand I made up my mind, for reasons based on previous experience, that if the Admiral made any scene I should keep complete silence, reserving my explanation until later. The Admiral was indeed furious, asking me why the port ladder was not ready in spite of orders which he had given the Flag Lieutenant more than two hours ago and he concluded by ordering me to "see to it myself". I replied, "Aye aye Sir", and took charge personally.

'5. In a few moments I reported to the Captain that the barge was coming alongside and briefly explained what had happened. The ship was now swinging to port and although the port side was, for the time, the lee side, the ship was bearing down on any boat alongside the port side. It would certainly have been against my judgement to have used this side or the other side until the ship had swung nearly to the wind. There was considerable swell, a rather choppy sea and sufficient wind to cause white horses.

'6. The disembarkation was, however, carried out without damage and the barge shoved off at 2115. (The anchor was let go at 2103).

'7. I informed Lieutenant Phillips that I was satisfied with the way in

45

which he had carried out my orders and that I took full responsibility for the arrangements which, as far as I know, were exactly as I had ordered, viz. starboard accommodation ladder completely ready for lowering, a Jacob's ladder, boat rope, heaving lines, fenders and yardarm group instantly ready for either side, with plenty of officers and men standing by.

'8. In the course of subsequent enquiries as to what had led up to the Admiral's fury, I learned incidentally that he had told the Captain in a loud voice and heated manner, in the presence of seamen moreover, that he was fed up with the ship. My informant stated that he felt disgusted at what he considered was the insulting behaviour of the Admiral to the Captain, although he did not hear in detail the rest of the abuse.'

Apart from the wording of the last paragraph perhaps, Daniel had phrased his letter as any senior and highly experienced officer might. Unfortunately he had more on his mind. Collard was soon to conduct an admiral's inspection of his sub-division of the First Battle Squadron including *Royal Oak*. As usual it was going to be a thorough and arduous affair of drills, exercises and scrupulous eye-searching. Already Daniel was preaching the need for extra efficiency to his subordinate officers and ratings. At the same time he could not help feeling bitterly that Collard was making it clearer each day that he had little respect for his flagship and that the chances of the ship and her crew having a fair and honest report were almost negligible. And anything but a good report could damn Daniel and his hopes of promotion to captain. More deeply, maybe, he felt the anger and sense of injustice of any good seaman when his ship and her crew were unfairly stigmatized.

Daniel was an emotional man, a would-be actor, a hopeful playwright. The sense of drama was far too strong for him to resist.

He wrote on:

'9. This concludes my report on the events, but I consider it my duty to point out what serious harm is done by such incidents. On the last occasion great pains were necessary to restore the respect of the Admiral in the public opinion of the wardroom and of the lower deck, and I feel confident that this had been achieved. This occurrence, together with and emphasized by the insult before nearly 100 officers and men at 1745 yesterday, has had a very serious effect on discipline and morale. Among wardroom officers, those who had the mortifying experience of witnessing those scenes are inflamed with indignation, and all officers are deeply resentful of the humiliation to which they see that their Captain and their ship have been subjected.

'10. I myself, was not personally affronted by any words used by the Admiral to me, and my sole reason for representing this state of affairs is that I consider the morale of the ship the special care of the Commander, and I should be guilty of neglect and cowardice if I shrunk from asking that a protest should be made in the most generous but uncompromising way possible at your discretion. Apologies would serve no useful purpose, but assurance is urgently necessary that discipline, which must depend upon respect for rank, will not be undermined in this way.

'11. Moreover I wish to draw your attention to the inevitable apprehensions which prevail concerning the forthcoming Admiral's inspection. The ship is discouraged. My recent appeal to look forward to the inspection, thereby making it serve a useful purpose for the efficiency of the Service, has been reversed by the anticipation of vindictive fault-finding.'

An eminent criminal lawyer once said 'Dartmoor is full of men who have made statements'. He would have shaken his wig sadly had he been present when Daniel finally laid down his pen.

Before the Commander signed it he sought out five of the most senior wardroom officers and invited them to his cabin. When they had crowded in he read out the letter. 'For God's sake stop me and don't let me send it in,' he begged, 'if there is any doubt at all in your minds.' There was not a single doubtful nor dissenting voice.

When they had gone Daniel signed the letter and addressed it to Dewar for it was the Captain who had asked for his reasons in writing and Daniel naturally assumed that it was for his Captain's eyes only and that it would eventually come to rest in some confidential file. Then he changed his mind and instead of sending the letter by messenger he delivered it personally and asked Dewar how many copies were needed.

Dewar answered, 'My secretary is shortly leaving the ship. He is absolutely trustworthy. Give it to him to type.'

Paymaster Lieutenant-Commander Stuart Thomson Crichton, Dewar's secretary, was shown the draft letter. He read it and was extremely startled. Such a document had never come his way in his career. Without being asked, he saw the absolute need for confidentiality and typed the letter in his own cabin.

Daniel was in for a shock. For his Captain, that austere, remote Scot, a man who weighed every action carefully, told him that he had also decided on a line of action. After being cut dead on his own quarterdeck by his own admiral, he too had decided to write a letter. His was to be to Collard's immediate superior, Vice-Admiral John Kelly, Commanding the First Battle Squadron. He said that he intended to enclose Daniel's letter with his own. After his first astonishment, there is no evidence that the Commander ever objected.

It is much more significant that, on first reading Daniel's emotional letter originally intended for his eyes alone, Dewar the pedant, a man used to the orthodox ways of flag officers, never expressed any objection to its style and passionate language nor suggested even mildly that his subordinate should amend it and tone it down before others saw it.

Later, it is true, he did make some gentle suggestion of the sort but by that time Daniel, bolstered by the thought of his Captain's support, would not hear of the idea.

6

Court of Inquiry

Dewar's letter to vice-admiral john kelly was even longer than his Commander's report to him. It stretched to almost four pages and contained twenty-three neatly numbered paragraphs. It was also more restrained.

Dated 8 March, it opened.

'Sir,

I have the honour to submit the following letter in accordance with the procedure laid down in King's Regulations and Admiralty Instructions Article 9. I am extremely loathe to make a complaint against my superior officer, Rear-Admiral St George Collard, CB, DSO, but I have no alternative as his behaviour is calculated to undermine not only my own position but the general discipline of the ship which I have the honour to command. After careful consideration I have decided that this is the only course open to me and the incidents complained of are therefore described below.'

Out of the remaining twenty-two paragraphs, the first half, exactly eleven of them, dealt with the ship's dance and what Collard had called Bandmaster Barnacle.

Dewar ended by dealing with the incident on 6 March.

'On the following afternoon the Rear-Admiral returned to the ship at 1745. The watch was fallen in on the quarterdeck ready to work the derrick and hoist in the barge. Entirely ignoring the Commander, Duty Lieutenant-Commander and the Officer of the Watch who were stationed there to receive him, he shouted for men to get down the ladder, attend boat ropes etc. After completing the disembarkation of his gear, he ordered the barge ashore and walked past me without returning my salute. His general attitude and demeanour had every appearance of a studied insult to me in the presence of a large number of officers and men.'

When his secretary, Lieutenant-Commander Crichton, returned to him with a typed copy, now bearing a large 'Secret' stamp at its head, Dewar read it and pondered over the subscription on the first page. This read:– 'The Vice-Admiral Commanding, First Battle Squadron'. And underneath, '(Copy to Rear-Admiral)'. He altered that last line to '(Through Rear-Admiral)' and initialled the change. This cannot have been a casual afterthought. Dewar was not that sort of man. He had a rational and methodical mind and was not given to sudden whims. What that alteration meant was that instead of Collard simply reading and noting both Dewar's and Daniel's letters, he would also have to take them personally to his own superior. A clear case of twisting the knife!

Both letters were signed by their authors on the forenoon of Friday, 9 March, the day before the Combined Exercises with the Home Fleet were to begin.

They were put into a large buff envelope marked 'Complaints for the Vice-Admiral'; the envelope was sealed and at about two o'clock that afternoon, Dewar, his cap tucked smartly under his arm, stepped into the day cabin where Collard was attending to some paperwork, helped by his secretary. He placed the envelope on the Admiral's desk and left.

Hardly a word was exchanged.

Dewar gone, Collard read both letters. It took some time and then more time for thought. He must have been acutely aware that if the complaints reached Vice-Admiral John Kelly then action would have to be taken. Action from which he, particularly as the newest and most junior flag officer in the Royal Navy, could not possibly escape unscathed. Fellow officers wondered for long afterwards why Collard had not pressed that bell on his desk and smartly requested the attendance of Dewar and Daniel. Surely, even at that late date, a long and private talk with his subordinates, a pledge of better understanding from the three men, perhaps some sort of an apology all round and the air would have been cleared and those letters torn up.

Collard did nothing of the sort. Instead he speculated with his secretary as to the chances of catching Vice-Admiral Kelly that afternoon, then changed his mind and decided to leave things until the morning.

So at quarter past nine on Saturday morning, while *Royal Oak* and every other ship in crowded Grand Harbour were abustle with all the activity of preparing for sea and the annual Spring Exercises for which they had been so long in training, while lighters were still alongside and ammunition and stores were still coming on board, Rear-Admiral Collard was piped over the side and into his barge which headed straight for Kelly's own flagship, HMS *Warspite*.

The sight of the stocky, sharp-nosed figure of his subordinate at that moment was obviously a vision Vice-Admiral Kelly could have cheerfully foregone. The weight of command was heavy when there were only seven hours of preparation left before his battle squadron of great ships left harbour and headed for sea. Still, he took Collard into his day cabin, read the letters and then talked for the best part of an hour. It was later alleged that Collard spent most of this time not so much defending his own actions, but vilifying his subordinate officers for their lack of loyalty and support.

Collard always angrily denied this. But even if he had it would have served him little good. If it was in his mind or the minds of Dewar and Daniel, as it most probably was, that John Kelly would simply shrug his shoulders and suggest that, as time was pressing and the three of them were clearly not getting on together, then the simple answer would be for Collard to shift his flag into another vessel of the First Battle Squadron, then it was a great mistake.

Kelly was not only a staunch ally of the Commander-in-Chief, but he also knew his master well. Keyes ruled the Mediterranean Fleet. He ruled it and ran it. Nothing was too small or insignificant for his attention . . . certainly not a roaring quarrel between three senior officers. Keyes would have to be told.

Kelly called for his own barge and at 10.30 a.m. was boarding HMS *Queen Elizabeth*, the C-in-C's flagship.

As Kelly had suspected, Sir Roger Keyes was outraged. Already the Spring Exercises had been cut short because the Atlantic Fleet had to return home to England at the behest of King George V himself, in time to be reviewed by, of all people, a prince of Afghanistan. This had displeased him greatly. And now these letters!

He remembered asking Kelly to find out whether relations between Collard and his Flag Captain were strained. That was only a few weeks before when Collard was acting as director of the war games room. As the Rear-Admiral and the Commander-in-Chief shared very much the same ideas as to how a war at sea should be conducted, that is, as it always had been, Collard stood high in his regard.

51

And Keyes recalled how, at that very war game, Dewar had seized the opportunity to expound his theory of tactics which many of his seniors considered an attempt to teach them to suck eggs. To prove his point Dewar had cited British naval actions in the late war. Keyes had been highly offended. As one of the senior officers in that war it was not only implied criticism of himself but also of his fellow flag officers, especially his great friend and sponsor, Admiral of the Fleet Earl Beatty. And to make such remarks in front of junior officers who were present in the Games Room – it had all been most deplorable. Keyes also remembered how angry and resentful Dewar had looked when Collard had closed the exercise and shut up his Flag Captain.

Whatever decision the C-in-C reached over this latest development, and there is no doubt at all that he would feel in all honesty that it would be for the good of the Service, it was equally plain where his sympathies stood.

But now, caged in his cabin aboard *Queen Elizabeth*, Keyes was in a quandary. It was obvious the three men could not stay together in the same ship, just as it was equally obvious that there would have to be a prompt investigation. There was far too much talk about weakening discipline in those letters for his liking.

There was nothing for it, a Court of Inquiry would have to be held – and smartly. This meant that the Combined Fleet Exercises would have to be held back. But if they were not to be ruined, sailing could not possibly be delayed beyond six o'clock on Monday morning.

So he ruled that the court should sit in under three hours' time – at half past one that Saturday afternoon. He ordered that the board was to consist of Kelly himself and Rear-Admirals W.H.D. Boyle and the Hon. H. Meade of the First and Third Cruiser Squadrons. To avoid unnecessary speculation the inquiry would be held at The Castille, a tall, half-shuttered building, once a hostel-cum-barracks-cum-church of the Knights of Malta, and more recently a place of naval staff meetings. If the Court were held, in the usual fashion, aboard ship, it would attract far too much attention.

It was obvious from the start what Keyes expected the verdict to be. In his own strongly worded opinion, he had already decided that both Dewar's and Daniel's letters were utterly improper. As for putting him in such a situation just before the Fleet sailed, it was altogether unpardonable.

Before Kelly left to set about assembling the inquiry, Keyes, in a most ominous voice, asked him to find out at the inquiry whether Dewar had consulted or sought the advice of any senior officer before taking a step that was bound to have serious consequences.

It was somewhere between half past twelve and a quarter to one on Saturday afternoon when Dewar and Daniel were first told that they were to face a Court of Inquiry within two hours.

The hand-delivered memorandum to Dewar read:–

'With reference to your letter of 8th March, 1928, I have directed.

Vice-Admiral J.D. Kelly, CB.

Rear-Admiral W.H.D. Boyle, CB.

Rear-Admiral The Hon. H. Meade. CB, CVO, DSO to assemble as a court of inquiry at 1330 this afternoon, Saturday, to investigate the circumstances disclosed in your letter and to inquire into the general relations existing between the Rear-Admiral, First Battle Squadron, and his Flag Captain and Chief Staff Officer.

You are to take all reasonable steps to hold available officers whose evidence may be required.'

The memorandum was signed by Keyes himself.

If anyone can ever accuse a Royal Naval warship of being in a state of pandemonium, then there was pandemonium aboard *Royal Oak*.

Dewar's first reaction was to order Daniel to stop all officers' shore leave as he considered every possible witness important. Bandmaster Barnacle was to be commanded to stand by too, and any other of the lower deck ratings Daniel felt might make helpful witnesses.

Daniel hurried down to the wardroom and found several officers having their midday meal. He asked them to finish at the latest by five past one. Then he gave orders for all the waiters to clear away the dishes and be out of the place by ten past. Leaving a startled and wondering wardroom behind, he rushed off in a search for more witnesses.

He was back in the wardroom on the dot of ten past one, only to find that the waiters had not done as he had ordered. He blasted the Royal Marine corporal in charge as only the commander of a battleship can. Five minutes later there was not a dish nor a waiter in sight. Only then did he tell the exceedingly curious members of the wardroom that there was to be a Court of Inquiry. He was just explaining to them that every officer who could give evidence would be required and asking who had already gone ashore when Dewar sent for him.

53

Dewar wanted a list of the names of any officers who could bear out the contents of his letter. In order to obtain them he handed over to Daniel a copy of his letter to Vice-Admiral Joe Kelly, so that it could be read out. As it was marked 'Secret', no one aboard *Royal Oak* except the Captain's secretary should have seen its contents before, and that included Daniel.

Rushing back to the wardroom Daniel started to read the letter aloud to the gathered officers. After each paragraph he paused and made an impassioned plea for any officer who could support the allegations contained in it to have the guts to put his name forward.

He was not even half way through – remember, it was a long letter of twenty-three paragraphs – when a messenger arrived. Dewar wanted to see him again.

Daniel handed over the letter to *Royal Oak*'s First Lieutenant, Lieutenant-Commander George O'Donnell, to continue reading and raced off to see what his Captain wanted this time. Dewar said he could wait no longer. He was taking the picket boat and going off to the Castille immediately. He would send the boat back for the officer witnesses and they were to follow him at once.

Once more Daniel returned to the wardroom, this time to find that O'Donnell was still reading the Captain's letter with a fair way to go. There was no more time. The rest would have to remain unread.

Now there was a heated debate better suited to a group of women who have been invited suddenly and unexpectedly to a party on the lawn at Buckingham Palace – what to wear? Nobody in that wardroom had attended a court of inquiry before. Was it full dress and swords or what? The harassed Commander looked at the wardroom clock, cut short the argument and told them to pile into the picket boat as they were, reefer jackets and all.

Two very important potential witnesses were missing from the group. They were Commander Malby Donald Brownlow, Navigation Commander of *Royal Oak* and, being of greater seniority than Daniel, President of the wardroom mess, and the Reverend Harry Goulding, the Chaplain. They had already gone ashore. But somehow a message reached them and they found their own way to the Castille.

Brownlow was a particularly interesting individual. As third most senior officer aboard the flagship he had considerable power and a great deal of influence if he wished to exercise it. He could have poured soothing oil on *Royal Oak*'s troubled waters, especially as far as Daniel was concerned, yet there is no evidence that he ever aired a view or gave a single word of advice. Among all the flagship's officers, from Collard down, he was perhaps the only one who had felt all along that the situation would end in an inquiry.

As for the rest of *Royal Oak*'s potential witnesses, once they landed from the picket boat, they made their way as fast as they could to the Castille. Daniel even managed to get a lift in one of the island's few cars. All the same they didn't manage to arrive until quarter to two – fifteen minutes late. Not a good way to appear at a court of inquiry in front of a vice-admiral and two rear-admirals.

Bandmaster Barnacle was left to seek his own path to the Castille.

The inquiry lasted for over six hours but it did not take all that time for the court to discover that the relationship between Admiral and Flag Captain was beyond repair.

Dewar was the first witness but from time to time, as he was questioned, Collard was invited to comment on his evidence and this soon led to high words.

A great deal was made of the incident at the dance and the fact that it had taken Dewar so long to drag the matter up again. This gave Kelly the opportunity to put the question that Roger Keyes had told him to ask.

'Before going on with this,' said Kelly, 'will you tell me, Captain Dewar, whether you have ever sought the advice of any senior officer before taking the serious step of writing this letter which forms the subject of the inquiry?'

Dewar answered, 'I consider that my letter takes the form of reporting to my senior officer.'

Kelly scowled. 'Two months after the event?'

While still pursuing Dewar as to the advisability of discussing affairs aboard *Royal Oak* with someone higher in rank, Kelly suddenly stopped and said, 'I should like to ask Rear-Admiral Collard – what have been the relations between you and your Flag Captain? Have you any reason to be dissatisfied with him?'

Collard did not hold back. 'I was not able to choose my Flag Captain. I was practically made to take Captain Dewar. I had a letter from the Naval Secretary asking me to take him and saying that if I did not, it would be very difficult to place him. I replied that I had no objection but requested him not to tell Captain Dewar that I had [not] asked for him, and when the First Lord wrote saying that he proposed to appoint Captain Dewar as my Flag Captain I did not object. I did not then know

Captain Dewar, although I had met him once or twice. As regards personal relations between myself and my Flag Captain they have been extremely difficult from the first day I joined. My Flag Captain has never tried to be in any way friendly with me. He has held himself aloof from me in every way, hardly ever spoken to me at meals. I have always, at the back of my mind, felt he was disloyal to me. It is a hard thing to prove but I have always felt that my Flag Captain would never raise a finger to help me if I were in difficulties.'

He went on to cite the instance only two nights earlier, when *Royal Oak* and *Ramillies* had been ordered to change berthing arrangements. Then Collard added: 'That is an indication of our relations. I feel I have never had help from him and he is utterly disloyal, and I have felt it, more or less at the back of my mind, that I must be careful of him. He has given me practically no assistance as Chief Staff Officer in the four months with me. Those,' he ended, 'are our relations.'

Kelly might well have interposed at that moment and asked Collard why, when he himself had questioned him after the war games, had he expressed himself as perfectly content with his Flag Captain. Instead Kelly said nothing.

Dewar in his turn, when asked if he wished to answer Collard's accusations, spared no words. 'I say that what the Rear-Admiral has stated is definitely untrue: there is not a word of truth in it, except that I admit that since the incident on March the 5th, up until now, I have not spoken to him. I dined once in his cabin and did not speak. On other occasions to say that I did not speak is untrue and such statements have been made up.'

Dewar was pressed hard by the Court, which really meant Kelly, for he was the main inquisitor. Question after question was asked about his loyalty to Collard and then, on his view of the tone of Daniel's letter. The Flag Captain stuck to his guns and supported Daniel in every answer.

Collard, although he had been sworn and cautioned, was not asked to give evidence formally. This is not surprising since he and Dewar had been allowed what amounted to a double act ever since the Court opened. Instead of Collard an unexpected witness was called, Captain Cecil Usborne. He was on Keyes' staff and had served with Collard as his assistant at the Admiralty about four years before.

The first question put to him was about his relations with Collard. Good or bad?

'My relations were excellent, could not have been better. I felt that

3 Captain Kenneth Dewar. "A quiet, haughty, somewhat withdrawn man". (p.20)

4 Commander Henry Daniel. "A competent officer, cool in action". (p.22) (*Leslie Gardiner*)

my chief encouraged and supported me and that we understood one another.'

Would he describe Collard as a difficult man to get on with as a superior?

'No. I certainly would not.'

In the course of conversation with other captains on the Mediterranean Station, had he heard that Collard was difficult?

'No. I have never heard the slightest breath of such a suggestion.'

That was the total of Captain Usborne's evidence.

Daniel was called next and he faced the same barrage as Dewar, especially over that phrase in the final paragraph of his letter: 'Anticipation of vindictive fault-finding.'

He gave one startling answer towards the end of his evidence. The Court asked him: 'Without in any way trying to excuse the use of the word (bugger), is it one which is used very seldom in *Royal Oak*?

Daniel replied, 'Yes, I do not remember ever hearing the word from officers.'

Anyone reading the official report of that Court of Inquiry would decide that it was simply a witch hunt and that Dewar and Daniel were the quarry. The truth is not so easy.

The fact is that the Court – even Kelly, who knew the C-in-C's mind and indignation – simply could not comprehend why they were sitting at all. Why had two senior officers like Dewar and Daniel gone to such lengths over a few piffling incidents? And if they had taken such trifles to heart, why on earth had they not had a quiet word with a more senior officer and sought his advice? Instead they had written letters that the Commander-in-Chief not only regarded as damnably inopportune, but, worse, had corrupted discipline by maligning their own Rear-Admiral. The Court was not so much hostile as incredulous.

Daniel went and the Chaplain, Harry Goulding, took his place.

He was asked: 'There is a statement in this letter that there has been a great deal of discontent on the lower deck. Can you tell the Court about it?'

Goulding said he could, and proceeded to do so. At one stage he said he had even heard the Admiral referred to as a 'Bloody little swine' by men using the smoking space just outside his cabin. After further questioning he did confess that the men might have been talking about somebody else after all.

Royal Oak's First Lieutenant, Lieutenant O'Donnell, came next. He was brief, confining his evidence to the fact that there was obvious indignation among the officers after the dance. They deeply resented the insult to the ship, the bandmaster and themselves.

Another witness, Lieutenant-Commander Husband-Clutton, deposed that while he had heard nothing of the goings-on during the dance, his partner had and she was very upset. She said there had been an awful row and the Bandmaster was to be sent home. The Admiral had used language which was very improper.

Kelly: 'Did the lady tell you what it was?'

Husband-Clutton: 'No.'

Now it was Bandmaster Percy Barnacle's turn. Barnacle, with his ingrained sense of respect, found himself standing at attention before three admirals. However, his ordeal was soon over. He swore on oath that the Admiral had called him a bugger.

'Were you upset actually at the word "Bugger" or at the fault-finding?'

'With both.'

'Which upset you the more?'

'Being sworn at.'

Towards the end of the hearing Collard's Flag Lieutenant, Burghard, now newly promoted to Lieutenant-Commander, testified. He could hardly have given his master a better reference. He said that relations between the Rear-Admiral and Dewar were hardly cordial. The Admiral was always very friendly towards his Flag Captain but Burghard did not think that Dewar always responded. Relations were correct but strained.

'Quite correct?' asked the Court.

Burghard replied, 'I do not think they should exist between admiral and chief staff officer.'

He went on to say that Collard and Dewar never shared the same bridge at sea. Dewar always went to the compass platform and that all communications were by voice pipe.

He added that for a short while he had been Flag Lieutenant to the Commander-in-Chief and things were very different then.

The rest of *Royal Oak*'s officers who had attended the meeting in the wardroom that lunchtime, who had so precipitously rushed to the Court and were now waiting at the back of the room to have their say, were never called. Just before eight o'clock that evening the Court was cleared and the findings considered.

At nine o'clock the three admirals comprising the Court joined Sir Roger

Keyes aboard *Queen Elizabeth*. They bore with them their findings already typed despite the desperate rush.

They read: 'The Court is of the opinion that the Rear-Admiral acted in an improper manner on the occasion of the first incident reported, and showed a lack of dignity and of a proper sense of his position. The second incident is considered to have been largely the result of the ill feeling that existed between the Flag Captain and the Rear-Admiral.

'The Rear-Admiral appears, certainly on occasions, to have been tactless and to have behaved in a manner any senior captain might take exception to.

'In these respects the Court considers that blame is attributable to Rear-Admiral Collard.

'2. On the other hand, the incidents would not in themselves account for the present state of affairs and they appear to have been made an excuse for the explosion of the resentment felt by Captain Dewar which had long been working up.

'3. The whole of this might have been avoided if Captain Dewar had, with the concurrence or otherwise of the Rear-Admiral, represented his point of view to the Vice-Admiral.

'4. The relations between the Rear-Admiral and his Flag Captain have obviously not been cordial from the outset.

'5. The Court is of the opinion that Captain Dewar's letter very much exaggerates the case.

'6. The Court feels also that Captain Dewar should never have accepted such a letter as that put in by Commander Daniel.

'7. Although there is no direct evidence of collusion, there is some reason to suppose that Commander Daniel was in one mind with the Flag Captain, and that the strictures on the Rear-Admiral were not entirely unwelcome to Captain Dewar.

'8. The Court considers that Captain Dewar is greatly to blame in the attitude he adopted after the first incident, as expressed in his own words –

"I therefore felt justified in taking no immediate official action, but it was necessary to reserve to myself the right of referring to this affair if, and only if, any regrettable recurrence should take place. With this consideration in mind no question of personal apologies either to the Commander or myself was entertained."

'9. The Court is struck with the fact that Captain Dewar, in his evidence, approved the letter written by Commander Daniel, criticizing the Rear-Admiral, and is of the opinion that his – Captain Dewar's – ideas of discipline are detrimental to His Majesty's Service.

'10. Finally, the Court finds that the tone and wording of Commander Daniel's letter purporting to give his reasons in writing for a definite incident are subversive and reprehensible to a degree.'

At breakfast-time that Saturday morning no one except Collard, Dewar, Daniel and the officer who had typed them had ever seen those two letters. Nor had anyone the vaguest idea what had been going on aboard *Royal Oak*. Now, less than twelve hours later, all three officers had been tried, examined and a hasty verdict delivered, typing errors and all. It was a great tribute to naval efficiency.

Aboard his own flagship Keyes stood in his day cabin, looking out at the lights and the grim outline of his Mediterranean Fleet and considered the sentence.

7

'Your Flag is to be Struck'

KEYES HAD A CONSIDERABLE PROBLEM. By the time he had read the Court's findings, or, from what one knows of the man, long before that, he had made up his mind that under no circumstances were Collard, Dewar and Daniel to remain in *Royal Oak* a moment longer than necessary. The three of them must be out of their ship before she sailed on the exercises. Dewar and Daniel were easy to deal with. He had several choices of action there.

The Rear-Admiral was an entirely different armful of gold braid. Collard had been appointed by their lordships at the Admiralty and it behove even a Commander-in-Chief to pick his words and deeds carefully. This was an unusual situation for the forthright Keyes and he did not like it in the least.

That Saturday night he slept on the problem. The next morning as the deafening sound of Malta's countless church bells clanged, chimed, pealed or tinkled according to their nature, across the harbour, and as ships' companies assembled on quarterdecks in preparation for some lusty hymn singing, Keyes sent for Collard.

Though he admired the man, respected him and thought him a fine sea officer, that did not stop him from speaking out. He told Collard that he was going to recommend to the Admiralty that he be removed from his command, and he was sure that their lordships would agree. In the meantime and until he had heard from them, Collard would transfer his flag to *Resolution*, sister ship to *Royal Oak* and also in the First Battle Squadron.

But Collard would have none of that. He pointed out firmly that in view of the presence of the Atlantic Fleet and the consequent sensation his supercession would entail, he preferred to leave *Royal Oak* and the First Battle Squadron altogether and at once. What was more he was prepared to resign his appointment if it would make matters easier for Keyes and was in the Service's best interests. It was just the sort of blunt, instinctive and patriotic statement that he would make.

Stormy as he was at the trouble besetting him, Keyes was very touched. He had not been mistaken in Collard. All the same, he readily agreed, for it was an easy solution to a most difficult problem. But there was no time for sentiment in the C-in-C's day cabin that morning. He told his newest Rear-Admiral that he must pack his things, leave for England at once and report to the Admiralty.

In answer Collard made a simple plea. Could he have permission to remain on the island for a few days just to sort out his affairs and dispose of his rented house. More like the old Collard, he also pointed that, if there were to be a court martial, then he would prefer to be on the spot, rather than have to travel back from England. At the same time he made it absolutely clear that there would be no request for a court martial from him in order to clear his name. Time and circumstances could do that. In fairness to the man, Keyes had to agree.

Soon after Collard left the cabin a signal was transmitted to *Royal Oak* and all the rest of the Mediterranean Fleet: 'The flag of the Rear-Admiral, First Battle Squadron, is to be struck in *Royal Oak* at 0600 tomorrow, Monday, 12th March, 1928'.

Keyes wasted none of his precious few hours before sailing on Dewar and Daniel. Senior officers as they were, he had not the least wish to see them. They received their sentences in the bleakest fashion possible.

Two other signals were sent off from *Queen Elizabeth*. One was to Dewar. It read:

'I hereby direct that you are to give up the command of HMS *Royal Oak* and proceed to England overland forthwith, reporting your address on arrival to the Secretary of the Admiralty.

'This order is to take effect from today, Sunday, 11th March, 1928, and is issued in accordance with King's Regulations, Article 241.'

The second was to Daniel in almost exactly the same terse words.

Dewar read the signal with his usual habit of failing to show any emotion at all. He was as remote as ever. He merely asked his servant to pack his things and lay out a civilian shoregoing suit, and a further message was sent by hand to ask Mrs Dewar to do her packing too.

Commander Daniel reacted in an entirely different fashion but entirely true to that volatile character of his. He instantly ordered a boat alongside and headed for *Queen Elizabeth*. Once on board the flagship he sought an interview which the C-in-C had little option but to grant.

Now Keyes was not an especially imposing figure, even in his admiral's uniform. He had a rabbity face and a receding chin. On the other hand he was renowned for his courtesy and his charming manners. Those manners were not much in evidence when Daniel, cap under arm, stood before him in his day cabin and demanded a court martial to bring all the facts into the open.

Very likely it was all the hustle and bustle, the orders and counter-orders of putting a whole fleet to sea and then the postponing of the sailing, but neither Keyes nor his staff appeared even to have considered the possibility that, somewhere along the line, the question of court martial might crop up.

When Collard had mentioned it earlier that morning and also foresworn the idea, it seems to have been the first time it had been mentioned. Now here was Daniel demanding his rights as an officer to be put on trial. Keyes was violently opposed to the very idea. In his own words, he simply could not think of a charge which could be framed to encompass the enormity of Daniel's behaviour. He thought the whole thing a ploy for Dewar and Daniel to court the maximum publicity. What was more, it was publicity the Royal Navy most assuredly did not want.

But Keyes did not have to explain all this. There was a ready excuse at hand. Thanks to Dewar and Daniel and their confounded letters, the Annual Exercises had already been delayed. There was no question of any more time being wasted for the sake of a court martial. If Dewar and Daniel wanted one, then they would have to ask the Admiralty when they got home. Nor was there any question of Daniel being allowed time in Malta to settle his own affairs or deal with his rented house, nor of him having a chance to say goodbye to his theatrical friends ashore. Both Captain and Commander had to be off the island that night!

Perhaps they were lucky at that. Sir Roger Keyes had thought deeply about putting them both under arrest, either aboard another ship or in HMS *Egmont*, the nearby shore station.

Despite the pressure of passing time before the combined fleets met at sea and the fact that he had to act quickly, Keyes was well aware that he was acting in a very high-handed fashion, and in Collard's case, completely usurping the powers of the Board of Admiralty.

Keyes was nobody's fool. He fully realized that his ambitions to become First Sea Lord and an admiral of the fleet might even be affected by the situation. So he devised a splendid explanation in preparation for the moment when he was bound to be challenged. It was as follows: he had considered it impracticable to telegraph a summary of all the evidence, facts and considerations that were available to him; that any such summary would be liable to misinterpretation and would be insufficient for the Board to make a decision. The full report, consisting of hundreds of groups of cypher, could not possibly have been sent before Sunday evening and he would have sailed before a reply could be received. Icing the cake of his explanation and remembering Whitehall's affection for long weekends, he was to add that he felt that, in any case, it would be improper and unfair to attempt to shift the responsibility on to those members of the Board who could be reached on a Sunday.

Keyes was confident that he had cleared his own personal yardarm.

Gaps had to be filled; it was time for two more signals:

'Captain E.C.B.S. Osborne, DSC, from *Egmont* to *Royal Oak* in command vice Dewar, (Temporary).

'Commander Guy L. Warren, from *Bryony* in command, to *Royal Oak* vice Daniel, (Temporary).'

Well over a day late, at six o'clock on Monday morning, Keyes led the Mediterranean Fleet out to sea. Beforehand there had been the customary and seeming confusion of the departure from Grand Harbour and its creeks – the din of shackles being hammered free, the noisy rumble of anchor cables clattering inboard, the sirens of the attendant tugs and a turbulence of churning water. Megaphones boomed orders, the high-pitched piping of the bo's'ns' calls repeated them, signal lamps blinked bright in the early daylight and hoist after hoist of multi-coloured bunting streamed out.

The Navy at Malta was off to play at make-believe war with the Atlantic Fleet. Hard play and critical inquests afterwards. There was no time to dwell on past squabbles and the fate of rear-admirals and captains. Not that the Fleet, apart from the crew of *Royal Oak*, knew very much in the first place. They were almost as much in the dark as the Admiralty back home and that was very dark indeed.

From now on any communications from Keyes to his superiors in London would be addressed 'HMS *Queen Elizabeth* at sea'. The Mediterranean Fleet had sailed over the horizon.

If Keyes and all his high-powered staff faced problems in communicating with England, there was one man who did not. He was a local journalist who made a little money on the side by sending the occasional telegram to London newspapers about affairs on the island. It was not particularly profitable as, on the whole, Fleet Street was almost entirely disinterested in Malta's goings-on but he thought that there might be some news value in the fact that the Mediterranean Fleet had not sailed on time. He had few facts to go on except that *Royal Oak* was no longer a flagship and that her captain and commander and their wives had left the ship and sailed for home. What made it more difficult was that there was no one he could ask, for Malta's anchorages were as bare of ships as streets are bare of taxis on a wet night. But he filed what he could, including mention of one or two of the most vivid rumours being spread around.

Guy Fawkes would have envied him. While Guy had failed to blow up Parliament, by sending off what he thought was an innocent telegram, Our Man in Malta lit a fuse that sizzled merrily right into the heart of affairs.

Although it was the beginning of March and close to springtime, Britain had been beleaguered by formidable snowstorms. Day after day the tales of villages cut off and cities paralysed had made headline news. Snow stories were just beginning to bore when in came this telegram from a considerably warmer, even though wet and windy Malta. Fleet Street prepared itself for a field day. Although neither it nor the Maltese correspondent had the slightest idea what had occurred, all the ingredients were there. An Admiral had left his flagship, two senior officers were no longer on the island and, above all, there was a great cloak of mystery. The story was obviously too important to wait for trained reporters to reach the island – that would take days – so the best had to be made of the few slender facts. And the popular press did its very best, or worst, depending on how one looks at it. Headlines flared. The closest to the truth was that the Admiral and his staff had fallen out; indeed had come to blows. The widest of the mark was that there had been a mutiny aboard *Royal Oak*. Wrong though it was, there could possibly have been some substance in the latter. Since the war the Navy had faced out and out rebellion over pay and conditions.

Each day the headlines grew larger and the speculation wilder. It is important to remember that in 1928 the British Navy was still the mightiest in the world and its troubles made universal news. In no time at all from Paris to New York Fleet Street's speculations were being repeated.

Fortunately, nobody asked the Admiralty a word. This was just as well, for the Board knew even less than the newspapers. It had not even had the benefit of a telegram from the correspondent in Malta. And Keyes, the man who could have enlightened them, was far away at sea in his flagship playing at war, the letters from Dewar and Daniel, the Court of Inquiry findings and minutes of his decisions all safely in his day cabin desk drawer.

That was the state of affairs until the night of Thursday, 15 March, five days after the Fleet had sailed, when the House of Commons was debating the naval estimates. London was snowbound, the night freezing and the hour late. Despite this, or maybe because of it, many members had stayed on. Unfortunately, as it happened, one of the few to go home was the First Lord of the Admiralty, Mr Walter Bridgeman.

There were two retired naval officer Members of Parliament who had taken it on themselves to guard nautical affairs, Commander Carlyon Wilfroy Bellairs, the Unionist member for Maidstone, and Lieutenant-Commander the Hon Joseph Kenworthy (later to become Lord Strabolgi), the socialist member for Central Hull. They had not gone home. Bellairs was first on his feet to ask the Government a question. The question he asked shows clearly how little even the politicians knew about the state of affairs in the Mediterreanan Fleet.

He said that he had learned that a statement was to be issued saying that the Captain and some of the officers of His Majesty's battleship *Royal Oak* had refused to sail under the Admiral, had been court-martialled and were being carried as passengers to Gibraltar. Could the Admiralty issue that statement as soon as possible?

In the absence of the homeward-bound First Lord, an ex-army officer, Lieutenant-Colonel Cuthbert Headlam, Financial Secretary to the Admiralty, rose from his seat on the Government front bench to reply. First, however, he had another important topic with which to deal – the making of historical sea films. He said it was the Admiralty's sound policy to assist in the production of such films, simply for the sake of naval accuracy. Besides, he added, the fees earned benefited the Service's sports funds. As for the matter of the *Royal Oak*, he could only say that the Admiralty had not yet sufficient information to enable him to give any answer or make any remarks on the subject.

The Admiralty urgently needed information. All it had so far was a garbled signal that had arrived on the Monday morning the Fleet sailed. It could make neither head nor tail of that. So on Monday afternoon it telegraphed *Queen Elizabeth* for enlightenment. The answer reached them the following day. That was the message from Keyes saying that the whole matter was too complicated and too long to transmit by radio. He had sent his written report by hand of officer, and it should reach them soon. Unfortunately, it was not soon enough.

Dewar and Daniel reached England first. Obeying Keyes' orders to the letter, they had embarked aboard a homeward-bound liner with their wives and hastily packed luggage on the Sunday evening and reached home by Thursday, only hours before Bellairs rose to ask his question in the House of Commons.

The moment Dewar arrived in England, he sent his wife off to their home in Kent and went straight to his London club, the United Services in Pall Mall, and that same day posted a letter to the Secretary of the Admiralty. He must have been composing it during the passage home for it was a very long letter. Its ostensible purpose was to inform the Admiralty of his whereabouts as he had been instructed. But it went much further than that. It read:

'This summary and ignominious removal, unless immediate steps are taken on my behalf, will be viewed as dismissal from my ship. Even before I left Malta a rear-admiral informed a post captain, whose name can be given if desired, that Rear-Admiral Collard was the victim of a conspiracy.

'The statement is of course, absurd.

'Put briefly, Rear-Admiral Collard was subject to occasional explosive fits of temper which were extremely prejudicial to the discipline of the ship and about which I felt bound to make a complaint. What statements were made about me by Rear-Admiral Collard I do not know, but I do know that Rear-Admiral Collard, on receiving my letter sent in accordance with the King's Regulations, had a private interview with the Vice-Admiral who was later President of the Court of Inquiry. The whole tone of the Inquiry convinced me that counter statements of some sort had been formulated.

'On the general defective procedure of the Court and its attitude, which made it difficult, if not impossible, to elicit the relevant facts of the case, I am forwarding a further letter. Apart from anything else, I beg to point out that the minutes of the Court of Inquiry cannot be accepted as either complete or reliable. From my own personal observation the paymaster lieutenant shorthand writer could not keep up with the evidence.'

Dewar was in a strong position here. For he had been sitting immediately next to that notetaker.

'I submit that I should have been given some opportunity of preparing a case. This I did not have. At 1.20 p.m. on 10th March I was told the subject of the inquiry and ordered to attend it at 1.30 p.m.

'The witnesses I desired to call were not called, nor was I given an opportunity of asking questions.

'I cannot believe that such a procedure can be regarded as correct.

'I have the honour to suggest that the question at issue here is:

'Can an officer or man be penalised severely without any charges being framed against him or without any opportunity of knowing them and answering them?'

Dewar went on to defend Daniel. Finally he requested an Admiralty investigation and if his conduct was found at fault then he wished to be tried by court martial. If neither, then:

'I shall trust Their Lordships to reinstate Commander Daniel and myself in my ship and to protect our interests and honour, which hitherto, we have had no sufficient opportunity to defend.'

He marked the envelope 'Secret' and it arrived by first post the next morning, together with one from Daniels also demanding that he be restored to his position in *Royal Oak* or be allowed to stand trial at a court martial.

So for quite a while that day their Lordships of the Admiralty were in the most awkward position of having two senior officers insisting on their rights without having the least idea what they were talking about.

It hardly helped matters that Walter Bridgeman, the political head of the Navy, decided to make a statement that very afternoon to the House of Commons before it settled down to the business of the day. He opened by saying he wished to refer to events aboard *Royal Oak*. He told the House that he had received only a wireless message rendered rather incoherent in transmission, but sufficiently decipherable to show that there had been no court martial. There had, however, been an inquiry affecting only two or three senior officers of the ship. He added that the Admiral's flag had been transferred to another ship, but he asked for patience until he was able to read to the House a written despatch now, doubtless, on its way.

As it happened, Keyes' officer messenger reached the Admiralty building while Bridgeman was still at the House of Commons. He explained his late appearance by saying that he had been delayed, though no one seems to know why. At least with the arrival of the messenger, although he had only brought with him a copy of the verbatim report of the Inquiry and its findings, their Lordships had some idea of what had gone on in Malta.

Considering that it was now well into the start of the traditional English long weekend, the Board acted with remarkable promptitude.

Late that Friday it issued a statement:

'A Court of Inquiry was held at Malta by order of the Commander-in-Chief, Mediterranean Station to investigate certain disciplinary matters in which Rear-Admiral Bernard St. G. Collard, CB, DSO, Captain Kenneth Dewar, CBE and Commander H.M. Daniel, DSO, were involved.

'As a result of the inquiry the three officers concerned were suspended from duty by the Commander-in-Chief, whose report has not yet been received at the Admiralty.

'Since the First Lord made his statement in the House today he has ascertained that Rear-Admiral Collard's flag has not been transferred to another ship, as he inferred from an earlier telegram, but has been struck and that he is still in Malta.'

Poor old Admiralty. As it happened and even as the statement was being issued, Collard was on his way home by his favourite form of travel, the overland train from Italy.

The next morning, Saturday, the First Lord was summoned to Buckingham Palace. King George V, the Sailor King, who was so proud of the Navy in which he was Admiral of the Fleet, inquired in his bluff and direct fashion what the hell was going on.

Sir Roger Keyes was not a name to conjure with that morning. At least not so far as future promotion to the Board of Admiralty was concerned.

To add to all else, a second letter arrived from Dewar. As before, it was marked 'Secret'. And true to his custom, it was a long one.

In it he complained once more that Collard had had a private interview with the President of the Court before the Inquiry opened, although it is hard to see how the Rear-Admiral could possibly have handed over the letters without seeing Kelly privately in the latter's capacity of senior officer. But Dewar was adamant that Collard must have complained about him.

He wrote in this second letter: 'Yet the Vice-Admiral, 1st Battle Squadron, sat as President of the Court without giving me the smallest inkling of any complaints made against me. If the finding of the Court leads to my final removal from HMS *Royal Oak*, I have the honour to submit that such procedure is contrary to the most elementary conception of justice.'

Later in his letter he protested: 'It seemed to me that the Court wished to make as little as possible of the actual complaints and to go off into side issues, such as "Did a man really mind being called a bugger?" Was the *Royal Oak* very particular? etc. The point was the attendant circumstances but when one witness suggested that the presence of ladies made a difference, he was told sharply to confine himself to the point.'

Obviously Dewar had decided that the request he had made the day before for an Admiralty investigation was out of the question, for he ended his letter by earnestly requesting a court martial in order to clear his name.

This letter was written on the Friday that Keyes' belated messenger arrived bearing the minutes of the Inquiry. But if their Lordships thought that the weekend would bring relief from this postal bombardment they were mistaken.

The next morning Dewar wrote yet a third letter, nearly four pages long. It consisted, in the main, of a dissertation on discipline.

Having posted it, Dewar left his club and set off for his home, 'Branksome', at Sevenoaks in Kent.

On Sunday a thought occurred to him. He sat down and wrote his fourth letter to the Admiralty in four days. This time it was short and to the point:

'Will you please inform me as soon as possible whether I am on full or half pay?'

Meanwhile Daniel, who was staying at his own London club, put on his top hat, put a flower in his buttonhole and attended a society wedding.

What weight Dewar's postal barrage carried will never be known, but, in spite of a spate of signals from Keyes offering the most vigorous objections and the fact that the Royal Navy was going to suffer a deal of most unfortunate publicity, the Board met on the following Monday morning and decided that Dewar must have his way. A court martial there was going to be.

That afternoon Walter Bridgeman, the First Lord, stood up in Parliament and gave a full account to an amazed House of what had really happened aboard *Royal Oak*. He also announced that both Dewar and Daniel would be granted their courts martial.

If the poor man thought that at last he was able to shut up the popular Press with its wild stories of mutiny and imprisonment, then he was right. But when it regained its breath Fleet Street burst out anew with hilarity at the thought of the Rear-Admiral and the Bandmaster.

A really rousing storm in a teacup was, in their eyes, the perfect medicine for snowbound readers. The morning after Bridgeman had made his statement the London *Evening Standard* street-sellers were having a busy time. Low, the famous cartoonist, had produced a half-page drawing of the Board of Admiralty in full gold braid, playing drums and a piano on the quarterdeck of *Royal Oak*, being led by a red-faced Rear-Admiral puffing at a trombone and accompanied by a row of captains with saxophones. The caption read 'Syncopated Discipline Recital on the *Royal Oak*.'

The Admiralty saw it and winced. There still exists an interdepartmental memorandum which reads: 'Enclosing cartoon from the *Evening Standard* of March 20th, 1928. Request Admiralty action'. Wisely, no action was taken.

The story was once more embraced by the world's Press. The French laughed loudest of all.

Roger Keyes was a gallant officer, his record of bravery can never be denied. He was also a stickler for detail. Even at sea, involved in complicated exercises with the Combined Fleets and trying to stop the thrice-damned, pusillanimous Admiralty from granting courts martial to two men whose account of affairs was bound to make the Royal Navy a laughing stock, he remembered one small item and sent for his secretary.

One more memorandum was fired off to the Secretary of the Admiralty: 'I have reported by telegram the circumstances under which the flag of Rear-Admiral Collard was struck and I have authorized that the expenses of his journey to England shall be charged to the public account, in the same way as if he had been superceded in the ordinary course.

'Captain Dewar and Commander Daniel left Malta on Sunday night, 11th March; I have given no instructions as to the expenses of their journey, but I directed that they are to proceed to England forthwith and I consider that their expenses should be charged to the public account.'

As soon as the coming courts martial were announced Dewar left Kent and travelled back to London. There he met Daniel to prepare their plans. There can be no question at all that Dewar wished to conduct his own cause. He needed no fellow officer nor civilian lawyer to plead his case and act as 'Accused's friend', for he was totally committed to the justness of his cause and to his ability to argue it.

Daniel, however, had a lawyer cousin and was just as equally determined to use his services. Perhaps the strangest aspect of all the odd incidents of the *Royal Oak* affair was that Daniel prevailed. Reluctantly his Captain agreed to accept professional help.

Now, there were barristers around who were experienced in service trials, who understood their idiosyncrasies and, much more importantly, knew the hazards that faced a layman surrounded by service tradition and custom. Daniel's cousin was not one of them. He was not even British, or not really so. Until he had taken out naturalization papers about four years before, he had been an American citizen.

Day Kimball was an interesting man. He was thirty-five years old, born in Boston, Massachusetts. He had been called to the American Bar and for three years served as Assistant Attorney General to Massachusetts. When his elder brother came to live in England Day Kimball followed him. His brother promptly attained distinction by standing for Parliament in the landslide election of 1924 and winning his seat. There was something of a sensation when it was discovered that neither he, nor two other successful candidates for that matter, were British. To regularize the situation they were quickly naturalized. Day Kimball followed suit. He joined Gray's Inn and was called to the British Bar in 1926. When Dewar met him Kimball had less than two years' experience of practising in English courts. And none at all of courts martial!

What is more, he was well on his way to becoming an alcoholic.

8

'Subversive of Discipline'

IT WAS ANNOUNCED THAT THE COURTS MARTIAL of Dewar and Daniel were fixed for Friday, 30 March, only eleven days after the Admiralty had dithered whether to hold them at all. They were to take place at Gibraltar. The reason for such apparently unseemly haste was simply due to the fact that, because of the Combined Fleet Exercises, more than enough senior officers to sit in judgement were conveniently gathered together in one place. Gibraltar was chosen because it was closer to home than Malta but still near enough to Malta to make any witnesses easily available.

As far as the two potential accused were concerned it was a time for hurried conferences between themselves and with their lawyer. The snag was that they did not know with what they would be charged.

This bothered Parliament just as much. Those two ex-naval officer MPs, Commander Bellairs and Lieutenant-Commander Kenworthy, one a Tory, the other a Socialist, put aside their party differences and had a field day at Question Time. Bellairs demanded to know the terms of the charges. The Parliamentary Secretary to the Admiralty replied that it was up to Sir Roger Keyes to frame them. He added that the Admiralty was anxious that the position of the officers concerned should not be prejudiced nor prejudged by the House or the public and he asked the members to show patience and reticence. That request did not get him very far.

Bellairs: 'Does that mean that the two officers in question are proceeding to Gibraltar without knowing the charges against them?'

The Parliamentary Secretary answered that it did not. They would be told before they sailed.

Bellairs: 'Then what is the objection to informing this House what are the charges to be made against them?'

The Parliamentary Secretary tried a new tack. 'Because,' he retorted, to the cheers of his loyal colleagues around him, 'it is not the custom, and has never been the custom, to divulge the charges in a court martial.'

Now it was Kenworthy's turn. 'Is the honourable gentleman aware that in this case, owing to the extraordinary stories that have appeared, the extraordinary accounts of this episode, and its rarity, it is very necessary that the whole of the facts should eventually become available to the public?'

To even more loyal cheering, the Parliamentary Secretary answered, 'The Admiralty see no reason why this court martial should be any different from other courts martial.'

Kenworthy: 'Is the Minister aware that we have got to go back over a hundred years for an example of a rear-admiral being ordered to haul down his flag, and in view of the rarity of the case, does he not consider that this is not an ordinary court martial and that the public will expect full information?'

This time he got no answer. Another Socialist questioner rose to his feet.

'Are these courts martial to be held on board one of His Majesty's ships, and if so, will facilities be afforded the public to attend them?'

The Parliamentary Secretary said the public would be admitted, but his questioner was astute enough to press him further.

'Can the Minister assure the House that the promise that the public will be admitted will not be rendered nugatory by lack of facilities for going aboard these vessels?'

The Parliamentary Secretary refused to reply.

If it had been left to Roger Keyes, then those courts martial would have been held in mid-ocean, preferably the Pacific Ocean, but then he did not approve of granting the confounded trials in the first place. He shuddered at the thought of the bad publicity that the Navy was going to bring upon itself, and his views of the conduct of Dewar and Daniel grew sourer by the day.

The Admiralty, on the other hand, particularly its political members, realized that blessed privacy was not for them. The public and, more importantly, its representatives, the Press, were not going to go away.

What were the charges going to be? The naval law branch and the Deputy Judge Advocate had no doubt at all. They were to be based on the letters of complaint that Dewar and Daniel had sent to the Vice-Admiral. Those letters stood by themselves. There was nothing more to be said. Admiralty regulations were clear enough:

'Every officer is strictly enjoined to refrain from making any remarks or observations on the conduct or orders of any of his superior officers which may tend to bring them into contempt.'

Way back in 1806, soon after the Battle of Trafalgar, an addition had been made to this regulation. It read:

'This [injunction] is not intended to prevent any Officer or any Person whatever from taking such measures as the custom of the Service allows to obtain redress for any injustice or injury done to them as directed by the 7th article of these Instructions or protection from Tyranny or any oppression he may suffer by the conduct or orders of his superiors.'

This amendment stemmed directly from Nelson who had argued for a long time that there should be some liberalization of the harsh regulations once necessary to preserve discipline when a ship could well be alone at sea for months, even years.

The amendment was soon removed when Admiral Lord Collingwood, Nelson's loyal second-in-command at Trafalgar, but a traditionalist to the soles of his leather sea boots, was in power. His argument was that it was entirely prejudicial to good discipline.

In sharp contrast the Army Manual of Military Law stated:

'A soldier cannot in any way be punished for making a complaint under this section, whether it be frivolous or not, and he ought not, for making a complaint, to be treated in any way with harshness or suspicion.'

True, Admiralty Regulations also catered for complaints from the lower deck, yet added ominously: 'But his officer is to warn him that, should there be no reasonable grounds for his complaint, he is liable to be treated as having made a frivolous or vexatious complaint which is an act to the prejudice of good order and naval discipline.'

As far as Dewar and Daniel were concerned, the Admiralty was absolutely sure that it was on ground as solid as any quarterdeck.

Day Kimball, in his new role of officer's friend, made an appointment with the Deputy Judge Advocate. They argued for over an hour to no avail whatever. The DJA was adamant that the letters themselves were sufficient proof of the officers' guilt. Nothing more was needed. Then Kimball received a very nasty shock. He discovered in the discussion that the Admiralty had not the least intention of calling Collard to give evidence. He would not be attending the court martial but staying in

England instead. The DJA ruled that he was not needed. The truth or falsehood of the letters was quite irrelevant to the charge.

Something had to be done. When Kimball reported to Dewar, the Captain decided to go over his head and seek the opinion of a more senior lawyer. As a result of the advice he was given, he wrote a stormy letter of protest to the Admiralty. He had an answer by return of post. The Board saw his point. They would send Rear-Admiral Collard for cross-examination.

The Deputy Judge Advocate disagreed and decided that the matter would not end there. Dewar made up his mind that the fellow was an out and out enemy.

He was not the only individual writing to the Admiralty with some heat.

Three days after the Low cartoon appeared in the *Evening Standard*, an ex-Royal Naval lieutenant, signing himself 'A. French-Brewster', who was staying at the Grand Hotel, Leysin, in Switzerland (*'Cure d'altitude, d'air & de soleil'*) penned an apoplectic letter, enclosing a cutting of the cartoon, It read:

'As one who had the great honour of being in the Royal Navy during the war, I beg of you to take action with reference to the enclosed. This matter is now 'sub judice' and as this paper has no notion of decency in its cartoons, and in my opinion has clearly committed contempt of court, it should be surely easy to get a perpetual injunction against them and the editor committed to prison. I write in this way as My Lords showed me amazing kindness and I hate to see the Royal Navy brought into contempt. It is purely a civil process and so they cannot yap about the freedom of the Press (the biggest curse of modern life).'

Dewar and Daniel, accompanied by their wives, sailed for Gibraltar on 24 March, a hectic ten days after their homecoming from Malta. Despite the Admiralty's promise to the House of Commons, they still did not know the charges to be preferred against them. In fact the Circumstantial Letter had not yet been written. This is the document that Admiralty regulations insist must be composed before a court martial is considered. It contains a basis of evidence on which charges may be brought.

Keyes, who, with his advisers, was to draft those charges, did not receive the Circumstantial Letter himself until two days after Dewar and Daniel had sailed for Gibraltar!

The two officers, their wives and Day Kimball travelled in the P & O liner *Malwa*, bound for India. By unhappy chance among their fellow passengers were Rear-Admiral William M. Kerr, CBE, who was taking Collard's post as Rear-Admiral in the First Battle Squadron – Keyes had recommended him – and Captain H.D. Hamilton and Commander E.S. Brooksmith, DSC, who were to take Dewar's and Daniel's places as permanent replacements for the two officers temporarily appointed.

It was clear that whatever the outcome of the courts martial, Dewar and Daniel were not going to get their ship back.

Also aboard *Malwa* was a very fair sprinkling of British and foreign reporters. Keyes was certainly going to get his publicity, however much he abhorred the idea.

The company of so many senior officers must have presented the master of *Malwa* and his purser with a pretty problem. In view of the circumstances, which of them was to dine at the Captain's table? Wisely, they probably settled for regular customers, army officers and such like, returning from leave to India.

Early on Sunday morning Dewar and Daniel had a poignant opportunity to reflect on where their futures might be heading, for, passing close by, came the magnificent sight of the mighty Atlantic Fleet, bow waves foaming and glittering, as it steamed for home at the behest of King George V, to prepare for a royal review by King Amanullah of Afghanistan. Incidentally, the review turned out to be a considerable disaster. The April weather was appalling.

Malwa docked in Gibraltar on the following Wednesday evening, several hours late. Dewar and his party had a strange and chilly welcome. Almost immediately on landing he was told that on no account was he to go aboard *Royal Oak*, which, with the rest of the Mediterranean Fleet, was now lying in the harbour. If he or Daniel wished to interview witnesses then they must do so aboard HMS *Valiant*, another battleship belonging to the First Battle Squadron.

Then the small party made its way to Gibraltar's best hotel, the stately, marble-fronted Bristol, where the Admiralty had reserved rooms for them. But they were turned away. It seemed that by an unfortunate oversight, Collard had also been booked in at the same hotel and was expected to arrive soon. Dewar and company had to leave and seek second best.

At eight o'clock the next morning all Gibraltar echoed and re-echoed to the sound of gunfire from the harbour. Down by the harbour itself the noise caused all work to cease. *Royal Oak*'s new rear-admiral was being given the traditional thirteen-gun salute as he hoisted his flag for the first time. Now it was Collard, pausing in his breakfast at the Bristol Hotel, who had cause to ponder on his future.

It was on this day that Dewar and Daniel were first told of the charges brought against them. Each officer faced two. Daniel, who was to be tried first, was accused of an act to the prejudice of order and discipline in that he, being ordered by Captain Dewar to report certain events connected with the departure of Rear-Admiral Collard from *Royal Oak*, addressed a letter in terms subversive of discipline. He was also accused of being guilty of addressing a letter contrary to the King's Regulations.

Dewar faced two counts of accepting and forwarding that letter.

From now on the two officers worked furiously, interviewing every possible witness they could find. The task was not easy. Even some of those officers who had scrambled into the picket boat in their haste to give evidence for the two men at the court martial were not quite so eager now. The storm was over, the tempers calmed, a new rear-admiral, captain and commander had been appointed, so why stir up old quarrels?

Fortunately for the defence, there were sufficient officers who felt they knew where their duty lay – Major Attwood of the Royal Marines for instance, who was still explosive at the slur laid on his Corps – and who were quite ready to stand up in any court and have their say on their old Captain's behalf. But the main trouble was that Collard, Dewar and Daniel had hardly been in *Royal Oak* for more than three months, and that is little enough time to bind loyalties.

Meanwhile Day Kimball came across a most unlikely and unexpected snag. He was taking Bandmaster Barnacle through his evidence when the Royal Marine turned remarkably stubborn. He was simply not prepared to say that there was nothing wrong with the band's performance on the night of the dance. In his opinion they were rotten. Kimball was taken aback. If Barnacle insisted in giving such evidence in court, then, while it would not excuse Collard's language, it might well explain his tantrum. Kimball spent a lot of valuable and fast-escaping time with the Bandmaster before they agreed a formula. If Kimball asked him in court how the band had played that evening, then Barnacle was prepared to answer, 'About as well as usual'. No more no less.

Rapidly approaching justice had not finished with Bandmaster Barnacle yet. As far as the public were concerned, and much to his displeasure, he was one of the stars of the forthcoming courts martial. Fleet Street took a photograph of him in Gibraltar. Unfortunately it was not a good one. Barnacle, who was fairly short, was pictured standing, with baggy trousers that were even shorter. The Admiralty took one look at the newspaper and promptly telegraphed Gibraltar: 'Get Barnacle a uniform that fits'.

Everyone concerned was anxious to have these courts martial over and done with as quickly as possible, particularly the officers and men of the Mediterranean Fleet. Exercises ended, the ships were due to sail on the following Monday on the Spring Cruise, calling at all manner of pleasant places. The first port was to be Barcelona and it was important that the careful organization in that city should not be disrupted. Given any luck at all and a firm president to rule the courts martial, then they should be over in two days. Friday and Saturday would be sufficient time. But they were reckoning without Day Kimball and Dewar and, come to that, the Admiralty itself.

On the Thursday, with less than twenty-four hours to go before Daniel stood trial, the local newspaper, which also published the *Official Gazette*, was given a hint to wait for an official announcement. The editor waited but no announcement came by the time he had to order printing to start. Later the paper managed to get a line in its stop press: 'Courts martial postponed'.

The atmosphere in Gibraltar, which was already tense and strained, became as filled with rumour as Malta had been a fortnight or so before. Some said that Dewar had resigned, others that Daniel had sent in his papers. Against that there were quite a number of naval officers and residents who supported the theory that Collard had confessed that it was all his own fault and had taken full blame.

The truth was that, at the last moment, the Deputy Judge Advocate, fearing the solidity of his case, had thought of two more charges to bring against Daniel. The first was that he had read publicly, to an assembly of officers in the wardroom of *Royal Oak*, from a document containing certain remarks which were subversive of discipline. The second was that the reading of the document tended to bring Rear-Admiral Collard into contempt.

These charges were only made known to Daniel at half past ten on the

Thursday night. Quite clearly he had no time to prepare a defence by the next morning. Grudgingly, and treated much less fairly than a motorist on a driving charge, he was given only twenty-four hours' grace to do so.

But all was not a matter of lawyers' conferences and drafted charges that Thursday. Sir Roger Keyes was starting the long process of saying goodbye to the Mediterranean Fleet, for his long-extended term as Commander-in-Chief was about to end. Four thousand officers and men from the Fleet, sailors, Royal Marines and, in their paler blue uniforms, Royal Air Force pilots and airmen who served aboard the aircraft carrier *Eagle*, marched to the racecourse in the hot sunshine and paraded while he took the salute. A seventeen-gun salvo crashed out from the ships in the harbour, echoing and re-echoing from the face of The Rock. Then came 'Rule Britannia' played by the Royal Marine massed bands. No one complained about their playing this time!

Standing closely behind Keyes stood his old friend and overlord, Admiral of the Fleet Lord Beatty, wearing civilian clothes and his rakish yachting cap. His yacht *Sheelah* had newly arrived in harbour.

Aboard her, apart from Beatty, was his wife, a couple of elderly friends and Loelia Ponsonby, a great beauty who was soon to marry the Duke of Westminster, one of the richest men in England. When Beatty had invited her to join them for a Mediterranean cruise she had leapt at the chance. She was a rotten sailor but the idea had seemed fun. She found that she did not altogether enjoy the company of Lady Beatty who was an American and daughter of Marshall Field, the Chicago chain store tycoon. Lady Beatty appeared to be extremely spoilt. Previously married, the idea of her appearing at Buckingham Palace, even though she was now Lady Beatty, shocked the Establishment. However, the Admiral was a national hero of such stature that the courtiers relented, even though it might be the thin end of the social wedge.

Temperamental as she was, Beatty seemed to take her moods in his stride, and, with his yachting cap well over one eye, would face the day cheerily and with remarkable aplomb. The yacht first called at Malta and spent the best part of a month moored in one of the harbour creeks while Beatty called on his old friends at Admiralty House and at the polo club.

The future Duchess wrote: 'I adored Malta. Quite apart from the streets seething with handsome naval officers, the parties on the ships and all the fun, it is a fascinating island . . . While I was in Malta the great topic of conversation was the *Royal Oak* scandal, surely the smallest storm in a teacup that ever made headline news. It all began because the Admiral who flew his flag in the *Royal Oak* was peppery beyond the limits allowed to admirals . . . Malta buzzed. The harbour was alive with little boats whisking backwards and forwards carrying naval officers to secret conclaves. Those in the know looked portentous. We outsiders were devoured by curiosity.'

'Peppery' seems to have been the favourite adjective to describe Collard. At least where women were concerned.

While the Mediterranean Fleet sailed on the Combined Exercises Beatty and his party cruised to North Africa. Miss Ponsonby later wrote, 'I have never seen anything like the wild flowers in Morocco, and Marrakesh would have been delightful if Lady Beatty had ever stopped complaining about the flies.'

The yacht turned up in Gibraltar in plenty of time for Beatty to attend Roger Keyes' farewell parade. As the Duchess-to-be, that frail sailor, said, 'I was only too pleased to be at anchor, particularly as all our friends from Malta had turned up for the court martial.'

The parade also made a pleasant diversion for the Press. For at least one day in that gloomy, overcast Mediterranean Spring, the sun shone. The Press, and how to cope with it, was a problem very much on the Admiralty's mind, fully aware as it was of the promise to the House of Commons that not only would the public be allowed on board the ship in which the courts martial would be held, but that there would be no handicap to them getting aboard. A simple solution was found. The aircraft carrier *Eagle* was given a dockside berth. Her huge, bleak, empty 'A' hangar would be ideal for accommodating any number of people. After a lot of hammering and sawing, the Navy even went to the length of erecting a lofty and substantial wooden Press gallery.

9

'You Don't Know
what you are Talking About'

Saturday morning came, and a miserable morning it was, overcast, misty and a drizzle in the air, weather that was to hang over Gibraltar all through the trials. The Mediterranean Fleet, reconciled to the fact that it would not be sailing for Barcelona on the Monday, settled down to make the most of the courts martial.

The only distraction was the news, just filtering through from home, that, out of a field of forty-two starters, only two horses had finished in the Grand National, then run on a Friday, and one of those had fallen at the last fence, and been remounted to come in second (and last). *Tipperary Tim* won at 100 to 1. *Billy Barton*, the faller and runner-up, was a mere 33 to 1.

Aboard *Eagle* the court martial board assembled behind a long, green-baize-covered trestle table, stretching athwartships at the forward end of 'A' hangar. Those distinguished officers would be protected from the weather by the overhanging deck above them. The Press and public had to make do with canvas awnings for shelter. Blustery shelter at that.

Opposite *Eagle* in the harbour, and only a couple of hundred yards away, lay *Queen Elizabeth*, *Warspite* and *Royal Oak* herself. The cruisers *Frobisher* and *Cardiff* were close at hand and the rest of the Mediterranean Fleet formed a grim and formidable background under the grey sky. A guard of Royal Marines lined the deck outside the hangar, for there were compliments and salutes galore that morning as the court met.

Nine captains in full dress, with gold braid, lace and swords, had been chosen to try Daniel. The president was Fischer Burges Watson of HMS

Cormorant, the shore establishment at Malta. With him were Somerville of the battleship *Warspite*, Egerton, Fitzherbert, Taylor and Landon, captains respectively of the cruisers *Calypso*, *Coventry*, *Delhi* and *Ceres*, and Benson, Legge and Clegg, commanding officers of the flotilla leaders *Broke*, *Stuart* and *Montrose*.

Paymaster Captain Herbert Stanley Measham, CMG, was acting as Deputy Judge Advocate of the Fleet. His task was not to prosecute but to guide the court and make sure that the nine captains did not transgress. He was not a lawyer himself but he was supposed to be well versed in every page of the naval 'Bible' – *King's Regulations and Admiralty Instructions*.

The court having assembled and taken its seats at the table, with the president at its head, Daniel was produced. He had already surrendered his sword. Now it lay with its gilt and glossy black scabbard, non-committally, on the green baize table top, neither pointing towards or away from him. In accordance with long tradition, it would lie in that position until the court had considered its verdict and Daniel had been summoned for the last time. Then, if the tasseled hilt faced him, he was innocent; if the blade point, guilty.

Following Daniel and his officer escort came the official prosecutor, Captain Calvert, DSO, of the cruiser *Frobisher*, and Day Kimball, who looked oddly out of place among the gilt and gold in his wig and black stuff gown. Worse still, his wig was a pristine, almost silvery white. Most newly called barristers do their level best to borrow, beg, or in even extreme cases, buy a wig more battered, more faded, in the hope that its obvious experience of court rooms will shelter it's wearer's lack. Yet for some reason Kimball was proud of his wig's snowy elegance. To the nine worldly-wise naval captains who comprised the court martial board, it merely advertised that he had practised for so short a time that it was most likely he did not know his torts from his malfeasances.

Finally the spectators were admitted. There were over two hundred curious naval officers, most of whom should have been somewhere else at the time. There were more than a score of journalists. The true civilian public, for whose rights Members of Parliament, over a thousand miles away, had fought so hard, consisted of Mrs Dewar, Mrs Daniel, five Gibraltarians and two small boys.

The court now assembled, the warrant from Sir Roger Keyes convening it was read out with its traditional wording, starting with 'Whereas' and ending 'Given under my hand'. Then the court got down to business.

Almost immediately Day Kimball fell foul of authority. Captain Calvert, the prosecutor, was asked whether he objected to any member of the court; he said he had none. The same question was put to Kimball. He answered that he had no objection to any individual member but that it was possible that, without his knowledge, some members might have seen the minutes of the court of inquiry. Paymaster Captain Herbert Measham, the Deputy Judge Advocate, rose and told Kimball, in headmasterly fashion, that he was out of order. He explained that the defence could not object in general terms. Any protest must concern an individual; that if there was any suspicion in Kimball's mind that any individual member of the court was not capable of acting as an impartial judge, or had seen the minutes of the court of inquiry, or for any other definite reason, then he could object. Kimball retreated.

Right from the beginning the barrister found himself in conflict with the court and especially with Measham. Whether the Service minds disliked Kimball's attitude and his American way of presenting his case – remember that he had been at the English bar for less than twenty-four months – or whether Kimball thought that a legal brain could make rings round a tableful of simple sailors it is impossible to say, but from the very first hour it was evident that the chill surrounding him was not solely due to the bleakness of the hangar in which the trial was being held.

Having had some experience of Daniel's lawyer cousin by now, Dewar had already suspected that something of the sort might happen. Even before Daniel was arraigned, he had decided to defend himself. Kimball could assist him, but that was all! The four charges were read out: the first two dealing with Daniel's letter to Dewar and accusing him of using terms subversive of discipline and containing criticism of his Rear-Admiral, then the later and hastily drafted charges of reading out publicly in the wardroom a document containing such terms and criticisms. Daniel pleaded not guilty to all of them.

Dewar's secretary aboard *Royal Oak*, Lieutenant-Commander Stuart Thomson Crichton, was the first witness called. He gave evidence as to typing Daniel's letter and the steps that he took to keep it from inquisitive eyes. Under cross-examination by Kimball, he agreed that the letter contained a good many statements of fact and that if those statements were not true then there could be serious consequences.

Kimball: 'Now, as a matter of fact, did you, in your own mind, question the truth of any of those statements?'

Crichton: 'No, not for a moment.'

Kimball: 'May I ask why?'

Crichton, who until then had seemed extremely nervous and had given evidence in a very low voice, suddenly spoke up boldly. 'Well,' he declared, 'an officer of Commander Daniel's rank and character would not put on paper facts which were not true.'

It was while this witness was giving evidence that Kimball and the Deputy Judge Advocate fell out again. In British courts it is the custom for a barrister to remain standing at his seat while speaking and usually to confine histrionics to the scratch of a wig, hitch of a gown or the twiddle of a pencil. Advocates in the United States have far more latitude to walk about, strike a pose, approach a witness or lean on the jury box. Kimball must have had something of a memory lapse, for as he got up to cross-examine Crichton he took a pace or two forward.

'Get back to your place,' barked Measham, as though he were addressing an errant seaman.

The next witness merely read out the regulations under which Daniel was charged.

Collard himself was called next. Unhappy Collard; although irascible and hot-tempered, he was not an insensitive man and he must have wondered as he arrived on board *Eagle* that morning in his frock coat and gold lace how many more times he would be piped aboard a warship and have a file of Royal Marines present arms to him. No charge had been brought against him, he was not the subject of a court martial, yet there was no gainsaying the fact, as had been stated in Parliament, that he was the first rear-admiral ordered to strike his flag for over a hundred years.

Collard, despite that war wound of his and his limp, refused to take a seat at the foot of the table and insisted on standing. He was going to be on his feet for a long time. After he had taken the oath, the questions he was asked by the prosecution were simple; all concerned with how he had received Dewar's and Daniel's letters and what he had done with them. Then Kimball got to his feet and started his cross-examination. He did not get far before being twice interrupted by Measham. The second time was when Kimball asked Collard if he did not feel that the contents of the letters would involve an inquiry into his own conduct. Measham objected that, before the defence went into Collard's conduct, they should make plain its relevance. In answer, Kimball made an earnest plea to the court. He ended by saying, 'The questions in regard to Rear-Admiral Collard's conduct are admissible without any question of discretion because they go to the credibility of the witness for the prosecution. The facts of his conduct are relevant because the truth or falsehood of the statements in the letters depends on that conduct and in the third place it is within the discretion of the court to allow the putting of these questions in order that the real purpose of this inquiry may be arrived at.'

With a great shuffling and commotion, the court was cleared for twenty minutes while the nine adjudicating captains consulted. After the Press and public had been called back in, Measham announced that the court considered that Collard's own conduct was not relevant to the charges against Daniel, but, in order to allow reasonable latitude to the defence, Kimball could ask his questions.

Following the midday break, Kimball continued to cross-examine Collard. Clearly he was trying to discover whether, when Collard took the letters personally to Vice-Admiral Kelly, instead of sending them by hand of officer, which, Collard agreed, would have been a perfectly proper thing to do, the Rear-Admiral had taken the opportunity to present his side of the story to the man who was certain to be president of any board of inquiry. The prosecution protested on the grounds that any conversation Collard had in his capacity as the Rear-Admiral of the First Battle Squadron with the Vice-Admiral who commanded it was privileged.

Kimball withdrew his question and tried another tack.

'When you took this letter to the Vice-Admiral were you with him for more than half an hour?'

'I don't know.'

'What would be your best estimate of the length of time you were with him?'

'I should say it would be rather more than half an hour.'

'You think it might have been as much as an hour?'

'I should think possibly I was in the Vice-Admiral's cabin about an hour.'

Then Kimball suggested that by taking the letters personally to Kelly, he had made it virtually impossible for the latter to preside at a court of inquiry with an open mind. Collard laughed. Kimball said, 'I am glad you find this amusing. We don't.'

Collard answered tartly, 'I do. Because you don't know what you are talking about.'

Kimball: 'Now, if these two officers honestly believed that your conduct justified a report – honestly believed it – wasn't it their duty to make a report?'

Collard: 'It is the clear duty, in my opinion, of my late captain to come to me personally if he has any complaint.'

'Had he never come to you on any previous occasion with this sort of complaint?'

'He had not.'

'Had he ever on any previous occasion when in your presence, made a similar sort of complaint direct to you?'

'Only if I sent for him.'

'On what occasion?'

'I sent for him on the morning of Saturday, 14th January, immediately I heard a rumour that I had used a certain expression towards the bandmaster.'

'I want to go back to the question I put to you before, which you did not answer. If these officers honestly believed that your conduct justified a complaint, was it not their duty to make one?'

'It is the commander's duty to go to his captain.'

'Please answer my question.'

'I am giving you a fair answer. It is the commander's duty to go to his captain and my flag captain to make a report to me verbally.'

'Are there no circumstances under which it is the duty of the flag captain to make a written report on your conduct?'

'I can see no occasion. He is *my* own officer, *my* right-hand trusted and loyal officer – or should be.'

(Time and again Collard stressed that word 'My'.)

'There is no incident, however disgraceful, on your part which would justify his making a report on your conduct?'

'Nothing without coming to me first.'

Later Kimball asked Collard, 'In your view was Commander Daniel justified, if he honestly believed your conduct required it, in making a complaint to his captain?'

Collard: 'Quite.'

'And you do not suggest, do you, Admiral, that he did not honestly believe it when he made it?'

'I haven't the least idea.'

'Do you suggest he did not believe it?'

'Yes.'

'You do suggest he did not believe it?'

'He couldn't have.'

'Then you are suggesting, I take it, he was acting from some improper motive?'

'I don't know what he was acting from. It was a most insubordinate letter.'

Tempers grew taut when Kimball tried to make the Rear-Admiral say whether he thought Daniel had acted honestly or dishonestly in his letter. First, Collard angrily appealed to the Judge Advocate that he was not being asked straight questions. Kimball persisted and Collard retorted, 'Why should I answer either? It is a mere trap.' But finally the lawyer had his own way.

'Do you suggest, or think now, that Commander Daniel was acting dishonestly towards you when he made that report?'

'I do.'

'Then that amounts to an accusation of disloyalty to you?'

'Entirely.'

'And that accusation is an accusation of a pretty severe crime in the Navy?'

'I should say so.'

'Commander Daniel is not accused of that crime in this court martial?'

'I do not know. I have not seen the charge.'

Throughout the cross-examination Collard, despite the invitation of the court president, still refused to take a seat. His mood was as unpredictable as an April day. One moment he was casual, almost offhand and vague in his answers, the next stormy and grim; his voice would rise or he would growl. He growled when he looked at Kimball and demanded, 'Don't shout at me'. On another occasion he bellowed at the lawyer, 'Will you hear my answer?'

This was when Kimball was trying to prevent Collard making his own prepared statement about his conduct on the night of the dance. But the president interjected wearily and pointed out that time was valuable and it would be better if the Rear-Admiral had his own way. The Judge Advocate, surveying Kimball, added critically that some questions had already been asked and answered four or five times.

Collard denied emphatically that he had ever told Dewar to 'bite' his commander. He swore that he had never used the word 'bugger' at all, only a mere 'bloody' once or twice – once to the Bandmaster when he said, 'Bandmaster, what is the matter with the music? No one could dance

5 Bandmaster Percy Barnacle. "A man who knew his place and never stepped out of it". (p.22) (*Barnacle family*)

6 "Get Barnacle a uniform that fits". (p.79)

7 The Royal Marine Band aboard HMS *Royal Oak*. Bandmaster Barnacle is seated centre. (*Barnacle family*)

8 "The Admiralty saw it and winced". (p.71). The Low cartoon which appeared in the *Evening Standard* on 20 March, 1928

9 *Royal Oak* leaving Grand Harbour, Malta, in 1928

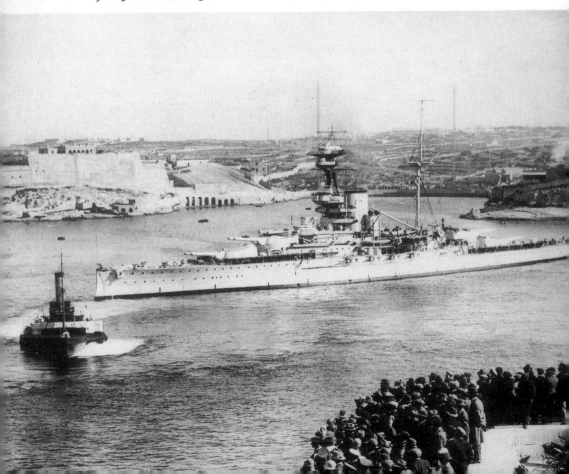

to that last tune. I don't think I have heard such a bloody awful noise in all my life. You must improve matters. You are not up to the standard of a flagship's band.' Afterwards he walked to the ship's side with Daniel and said, 'We can't have a bloody man like that in charge of a flagship's band. We shall have to get rid of him.'

Still on oath, Collard insisted to the court that that was the only swearing from him at the dance.

The cross-examination went on and on. By the time Kimball ceased, Collard had been on his feet for more than two hours. There was one final crossing of swords. When Kimball questioned him about the fact that he failed to salute Dewar in front of the *Royal Oak*'s crew, Collard answered contemptuously, 'A good ship does not depend on that sort of rubbish.'

After Kimball had resumed his seat, Captain Calvert of *Frobisher*, who was acting as prosecutor, tried his amateur hand at re-examination. Unfortunately for him, his fellow captain, the bristly Deputy Judge Advocate, showed a fine turn of impartiality after his criticism of Kimball, and regarded virtually everything he asked as a leading question and disallowed it.

Collard's flag lieutenant, Lieutenant Geoffrey Burghard, was another witness for the prosecution. Curiously, his evidence, though brief, was in Daniel's favour. He was answering questions about the scene when Collard wanted to go ashore in his barge. No, the Rear-Admiral had not specified whether he wished to use the port or starboard ladder, the Jacob's ladder was available and there were plenty of officers and men about.

At four o'clock the court adjourned for twenty minutes for tea, or something stiffer, and a smoke. On its return Paymaster Lieutenant Norman Denning of *Royal Oak* was summoned. He was the first of the witnesses for the prosecution to give evidence on the third and fourth charges against Daniel, namely those of reading Dewar's secret letter to the wardroom officers. He told how he was having luncheon aboard *Royal Oak* shortly after noon when Daniel cleared all the wardroom attendants out and asked for the names of officers who could give evidence on the occasion of the dance; of when Collard left the ship on 5 March, and of the occasion when the Rear-Admiral returned the next day. He described how Daniel started to read out the letter and of the interruptions caused by messages from Dewar. Kimball cross-examined him, but he did not get very far.

Kimball: 'You have told us quite frankly that the last part of this interview was extremely hurried, and that you really haven't a clear recollection?'

'No.'

'As a matter of fact the whole incident was hurried?'

'It was hurried.'

'Everyone was working under extreme pressure?'

'I wasn't myself because I wasn't working.'

'I said everyone concerned. I meant everyone who had any work to do was working under pressure?'

'They were not working. They were assembled in the wardroom.'

Denning said that the whole episode did not last longer than a quarter of an hour. He remembered Daniel saying that what he wanted was to get to the truth of the business and didn't care which way the evidence came.

Surgeon Commander Robert Cory also stated that he was present in the wardroom at the time. He remembered that Daniel, when he appealed for officers to come forward, said that he did not mind if the evidence they would give was not in his favour.

Lieutenant Lionel Haultain Phillips was Officer of the Day on 5 March, when Collard wanted to board his barge to go ashore. He testified that the starboard gangway was completely ready before *Royal Oak* let go her anchor. He agreed that the port Jacob's ladder or the gangway could have been used in the weather conditions as they were at that time, even while the ship was still swinging after coming to anchor.

Apart from extra evidence that the court granted permission to be called later, the prosecution's case was over.

Kimball rose and opened the case for the defence at exactly quarter past six that evening. He spoke for almost forty minutes in his American East Coast voice that seemed so foreign after the succession of almost identical clipped tones of the naval officer witnesses. He did not speak without interruption.

There are two sunsets – the one that God created and the other ordained by Admiralty. In naval eyes, God's sunset is a rather untidy and erratic affair and, so that its going down might be respected in good order and in unison, the local commander-in-chief decrees his own time. Hence ships in Northern waters might well celebrate the hallowed ceremony of 'Sunset' while it is still high over the yardarm. Roger Keyes had naturally dictated the time for the ceremony in the Mediterranean.

Both sunsets, heavenly and naval, are equally moving in their own way and apt to touch the heart and senses. At 1642 hours precisely a bugle sounded out from overhead in HMS *Eagle*, its call echoed from every quarterdeck of every ship of the Mediterranean Fleet, lying there in Gibraltar – a sad and wistful call. Simultaneously every white ensign was lowered for the night.

At the bugles' first notes, the whole court, including every officer spectator and every rating on duty, rose, faced aft and stiffened to attention, leaving Kimball, an alien figure in his wig and gown, in mid-speech.

Up on The Rock, under the overcast sky, the lights started to twinkle one by one.

It was almost seven o'clock before the tired court decided that it had had enough and adjourned until Monday, the day that the Fleet had originally planned to sail on its summer cruise. There was some muttering. If Dewar's trial was going to take half as long as this one, then the Fleet would be lucky to get away by Wednesday.

But not everyone in Gibraltar was grumbling. According to the *Gibraltar Chronicle* anybody in the place who mattered was consumed by an insatiable curiosity which had nothing at all to do with any court martial.

Before she had sailed for home and the Afghanistan Review with the rest of the Atlantic Fleet, the crew of the mighty battle cruiser HMS *Repulse* had staged a play called *All At Sea* written by a Commander Steven King Hall, for Daniel was not the only naval commander who fancied himself as a dramatist. Hundreds of guests had been invited (according to the *Gibraltar Chronicle* they finally numbered a thousand), but as there was to be a dance and a cabaret on board afterwards, poor King Hall had to cut a scene out of the first act, and the third act was not performed at all, to the frustration of the audience who went home wondering how the plot had ended. Perhaps, in view of the circumstances, this was just as well, for, entirely by coincidence, four of the leading characters in the play consisted of a cantankerous admiral, a harassed captain, a conniving commander and an unfortunate Royal Marine!

The play fared much better later. Revised, re-titled and with the writer Ian Hay as a collaborator, it had a long run in London's West End, as the comedy *Middle Watch*. It also became a film.

Now, all unaware of a very narrow escape, *Repulse* and her commander playwright had departed.

IO

'A Thumping Lie'

MONDAY WAS ANOTHER MISERABLE DAY and it was spattering with rain when the court re-assembled at a quarter to ten in the morning. Daniel, in full dress except for his sword, took his place in front of the nine senior officers sitting in judgement and bowed. Before Kimball could open his examination-in-chief, a warning shot was fired across his bows. Measham, the Deputy Judge Advocate, sternly pointed out that so far some quite inadmissible evidence had been presented by the defence and if he had not intervened it was only because he wanted to afford Daniel every latitude. This must have startled Kimball, whose own view was that the Deputy Judge Advocate had, very heavy-handedly, interrupted the proceedings a great deal too much so far.

The examination started with Daniel's version of the goings-on during the dance. He said that at first the Admiral had complained to his Captain about the number of ladies who were sitting out the dances. In turn Daniel had explained to Dewar that, while he had made sure four or five officers were available for each dance, he was having trouble with the rest of the wardroom.

He added, 'They point-blank declined to dance with other than their own friends and their own party.'

Then the Admiral, who by that time was very annoyed, complained about the band. He cursed and said that if Daniel was afraid to turn the Marines off the quarterdeck, he would do it himself. He then ordered Daniel to come along with him. When they arrived in front of the band Collard pointed to Bandmaster Barnacle and called loudly, 'Come here.

You stand here'. Then, before all the guests who were gathered around waiting for the band to start playing again, roared at Barnacle, 'You call yourself a flagship's band? I have never heard such a bloody awful noise in my life. It is like a dirge. No one can dance to it. Everybody is complaining. I will have you sent home tomorrow and have you reported to headquarters.'

Daniel added that Collard went on to repeat himself several times. Barnacle, who had stood strictly to attention during this tirade, answered, 'I will do my best, Sir.' Collard answered, 'Yes, I should think you would see if you cannot do a little better than you have been doing.'

The Admiral then turned away and, according to Daniel, made some remarks about the jazz band which, he declared, was better than the Marines. Daniel answered, 'Excuse me sir, that is not just. Whatever merits the jazz band have, they owe to this bandmaster who has trained them.' Collard cut him short and said in a loud voice, 'I won't have a bugger like that in my ship.'

Kimball asked Daniel if he could recall the Admiral's manner and tone of voice that evening.

Daniel: 'Somewhat the same as it was in the court on Saturday.'

Daniel went on to say that at eight o'clock the next morning he was on deck for the ceremony of Colours. After the band had been dismissed, he called the Bandmaster back and told him not to take the threat to be sent home too seriously, but Barnacle replied that he could never stay in the ship nor even in the Service after what had happened.

Later Daniel was sent for by the Admiral. When he arrived in Collard's day cabin he found that Dewar was there too. The Admiral immediately said, 'The chaplain has been aft here accusing me of calling the Bandmaster a bugger. Now you were with me and I did nothing of the sort did I?'

Daniel: 'I thought for a second because his manner was threatening and I said very deliberately, "If you ask me if I heard you call the Bandmaster a bugger, my reply is 'No'. But if you ask whether you referred to the bandmaster as a bugger in my hearing and the hearing of the band and of guests, including ladies – my reply is definitely 'Yes'."'

Kimball: 'Then what happened?'

Daniel: 'The Admiral got very angry. He said it was a lie – that he never used such a word. That such accusations could only involve a court martial about a flag officer and asked me how I dared say such a thing.'

Kimball: 'What did you reply to that?'

Daniel: 'I replied and repeated it three or four times during the conversation which went on, in these terms, "Nothing will budge me from that statement, sir!" '

Kimball: 'Do you remember anything else that you said of a similar nature?'

Daniel: 'Yes. I think it was when the threats of a court martial were being made, I replied, "Do you think, sir, that at this stage of my career, I should make these statements to you if there was left any possible room for the slightest doubt in my mind as to what you said?" '

Kimball: 'What did the Admiral say then?'

Daniel: 'I think I turned to the Captain at that point and said "As a matter of fact the Major is waiting to see you to lodge a protest because of what he considers an insult to the Marine Corps and I understand the Bandmaster has lodged a formal protest in the form of a request to leave the Service; to resign from the Service although it has been pointed out to him that it would mean chucking away his pension." '

Daniel then said that then Collard changed his manner completely and went on to speak of a court martial but now with a note of appeal in his voice. Daniel told the court that he said to Collard, 'Excuse me, sir, I have had more time to think this matter over and I have a suggestion to make which would prevent a scandal about a flag officer.'

He suggested that Collard should give him *carte blanche* to make the best redress possible to those individuals who, in his judgement, were really entitled to such redress. Grievous harm had been done and the logical thing, to Daniel's mind, was not to do greater harm by producing a scandal, but to make the best amends possible. He told Collard that if he agreed to this proposal then he would pledge his word of honour that, in his negotiations, he would maintain an order of priority: first to the Service, secondly to his subordinates who had a right to look to him, and thirdly to the dignity of the Rear-Admiral himself.

According to Daniel, the Admiral hesitated for a while and then asked Dewar for his opinion. The Captain said that it was not the correct manner of handling a formal request from the Bandmaster if it came forward. He also added that everything depended on success. As for himself, he felt that his responsibility was to the ship and that it was important that he could have some guarantee that such a thing would not recur. Dewar ended by saying that he could not think of a better suggestion then Daniel's.

The accused told the court that Collard then said some very nice things and wished him success. Then Daniel saluted and left the day cabin. The first person he met outside was Attwood, the Major who commanded the ship's Royal Marines. Daniel said that he told Attwood that he had managed to get a full apology from the Admiral and hoped that it satisfied his feelings about any slur on the Marine Corps. Attwood replied, 'I place myself entirely in the Captain's and your hands. I am damned glad not to have to press this matter but I must make reservations. If this thing, if anything like this occurs again, then I am going to refer to this matter.'

Daniel said he answered the Major by saying, 'That is perfectly all right. That is precisely the line taken by the Captain, and now our task is to turn this bloody awful incident to the advantage of the ship by gaining the most credit for the Admiral out of his apology.'

After that meeting, he went to his own cabin and sent for Bandmaster Percy Barnacle. First, Daniel hedged awhile until he was certain that Barnacle's main grievance was that he had been called a bugger. Then, according to his own evidence to the court, he told Barnacle a thumping lie. He explained to the little Marine that when the Admiral had been told of the Bandmaster's hurt feelings he had expressed horror and had directed Daniel to convey a sincere apology. Then Daniel went on to tell Barnacle, 'I think you will agree with me that is an extraordinarily generous message from the Rear-Admiral.'

Not surprisingly, Barnacle agreed and said he was very grateful.

Going by Daniel's own evidence, having lied to both the Major of Royal Marines and the Bandmaster, for never once in that evidence did he ever suggest that Collard had even considered an apology, he returned to the Admiral's day cabin and reported his successful mission. Seemingly Collard congratulated him on his tact and the bold course he had taken and said, 'Thank you very much for getting me out of a very nasty hole.'

What the nine captains trying him must have thought of the readiness with which Daniel owned up to such trickery, and whether they wondered what reliance they could put on the rest of his evidence, would be discovered later.

Daniel continued his evidence by describing his peace-making overture to Collard the next day by inviting him for a cocktail in the wardroom. After that, he said, his relations with the Admiral were very cordial and he dined with him twice. Cordial right up until March the fifth, when Collard had sent for his barge.

By now the court was becoming impatient. It felt that it did not need all this long-drawn-out detail. It stopped short of indulging in heavy sighing and taking out its watches but the President interrupted by saying that it did not need a great deal of detail.

Obediently, Daniel described the incident briefly and then went on to give evidence about the Admiral's return the next afternoon. He said everything was ready for Collard's reception with men on the quarterdeck waiting to hoist in the barge with the main derrick. The Captain had impressed on him only the day before that, in accordance with the Admiral's wishes, boats, particularly the large boats, were never to be left behind when the ship was out on exercise. *Royal Oak* was setting out for practice that afternoon. 'Then,' he went on, 'the barge came alongside and the Admiral jumped out. I took up my position at the salute inboard for manning the side. When the Admiral's head appeared level with the top gangway platform, he told the quartermaster to take his bo's'n's pipe out of his mouth and lower the boat rope. This surprised me.

'The Admiral then stood on the platform and proceeded to direct side boys – messengers – to jump down the ladder. He stood on the platform giving these orders in very rapid succession. I saw officers were handling luggage themselves, men were running up and down the ladder and there was a big commotion. Then the Admiral leaned over the gangway platform and said to the barge that she was to return. The Admiral came inboard. He walked straight past the officers who were at the salute – looked right through us – looked right through the Captain and cut him dead, and then walked aft to his hatch.

'There was the whole of a watch for exercise manning the derrick guys. Certainly more than fifty men were quite close and must have seen the whole incident.'

Kimball: 'Can you describe, in a single phrase, the general impression you got of the Admiral's manner on this occasion?'

Daniel: 'A deliberate insult.'

After giving evidence of events that led up to the court of inquiry, the inquiry itself and the order for him to leave *Royal Oak*, Daniel said that, once ashore, Major Attwood joined him to hand him his passport. In return Daniel handed Attwood a letter he had just written and which was addressed to the whole ship's company. Daniel wanted the First Lieutenant to read it out to the crew as soon as possible.

At this point Kimball asked him to read out the letter, but he was stopped by the Deputy Judge Advocate who asked to be handed the letter. He read it silently, then said that there was no objection, from a legal point of view, to it being read out in court, but added heavily, as a clear warning to Kimball, that he hoped the defence was sure it wished it to be read.

Now the court took a hand. Clearly trying to give Daniel a fair chance, the President, after glancing at the letter, interrupted and asked Kimball, 'Are you perfectly convinced that, in the interests of your client, he should go on? We ought to warn you . . .' He said no more, but Kimball took the hint and that letter was never read. Nor were its contents ever revealed. Yet, knowing Daniel's theatrical turn of mind, his farewell letter to *Royal Oak*'s ships' company must have been a most remarkable document. Little wonder that the First Lieutenant did not obey Daniel. In cross-examination the dance was referred to again. The Prosecutor asked, 'Now, I think you said that early in the evening after a number of dances, the Captain spoke to you and complained about the introducing. You explained to the Captain that it was due to the fact that some of the men would not dance except with their partners. Did you take any steps to try to get this situation improved?'

Daniel answered, 'I stopped dancing with the lady I was dancing with at the time, who I don't think I had ever seen before, and then I went round and I was almost rude to several officers and said, "Come on, you must dance," and even, "Have you got a partner? Where is she? Come on I will find you one," and almost took them by the arm as they were hanging back.'

The last question before the court adjourned for luncheon was: 'I understand Admiral Collard approached you and spoke to you regarding the band. Did he say, "I say Commander", or words to this effect, "the band is playing very badly. Something must be done about it?"'

Daniel: 'Well, something to that effect, sir, but in a very different manner.'

The afternoon session started where the morning had finished, with Daniel being questioned about the dance. Did he agree that the Admiral was justified in complaining about the band? Daniel allowed that the Admiral certainly had a right to complain about the band. He personally disagreed with the Admiral but he did not dispute that it was Collard's honest opinion.

'Did the Admiral remark to you that the Bandmaster was taking no interest in the conducting of the band?'

'I think that remark was made at the interview with the Bandmaster, to the Bandmaster.'

'Did he appear to be conducting the band with vigour and so on?'

'The Bandmaster is not one of these violent conductors ever. He is ol a very quiet type which seems to be successful with that band.'

It transpired during the cross-examination, and according to Daniel, that on the Saturday morning after the dance, when he, Collard and Dewar, had been together in the Admiral's day cabin, Collard had proposed sending for the Bandmaster there and then. He had said, 'If you like I am prepared to have the Bandmaster here and apologize to him.'

Why Daniel should suddenly produce so important a piece of evidence when he had completely omitted it in his main examination is most extraordinary.

He was then asked if the Admiral ever admitted calling Barnacle a bugger.

'Not in so many words,' answered the Commander, 'but by what I concluded, he did. Because I can conceive of no other explanation to account for his conduct – his threatening action when I came in – the complete change in his demeanour when it was clear this fact was substantiated by witnesses, and finally by his telling me I was to have *carte blanche* to convey or make such redress in my discretion as I thought fit.'

The Prosecutor asked: 'You explained that on the Sunday following, at church time, you observed the whole ship's company were looking hard at the Admiral and yourself. How do you come to that conclusion?'

'Because when the Admiral was about to go down the hatch I was standing there and was conscious of the gaze of all hands.'

'Was there anything unusual in that?'

'Yes, in the way they were looking. Their whole gaze was intently fixed on us.'

'What do you imagine was in their minds?'

'That they knew there had been a scene at the dance and they were watching carefully exactly what the relations between the Commander and the Admiral were.'

It was at this point that Daniel got himself into something of a tangle. He stated in cross-examination that when he wrote his letter of explanation, he had assumed it was for Dewar and not for Collard. Dewar had asked for his reasons in writing as to why there had been so much fuss about getting the Admiral ashore in his barge. It was an unusual request, but, then, it had been an unusual incident.

The prosecution then asked why his evidence differed from that he gave at the court of inquiry and read out the minutes in which Daniel clearly stated that Dewar had told him the Admiral wanted his reasons in writing. Daniel answered that he had hoped that the Admiral would see the letter, every word of it, so that he would realize what a very serious state of affairs had arisen. He explained that he had had some trouble in drafting the letter.

'With your position and experience you know how to address a letter to your captain and finish it off?'

'Yes, but it was a very peculiar letter.'

'Then you do agree that your letter, which you describe as peculiar, was going beyond what you had been ordered to report on?'

'Undoubtedly it was. I knew that.'

'Then you agree you did not carry out the orders you were given?'

'I don't agree to that. I agree that I exceeded the orders I was given.'

'You brought in extraneous matters which were not in the orders you were given?'

'Yes. I have never denied that.'

The prosecution then led Daniel to the day when Collard was supposed to have failed to salute and to have cut his officers dead. He was asked if Collard had saluted the quarterdeck. Daniel said he never saw him. He could not swear that he did not. But his impression was that Collard did no such thing.

Prosecutor: 'If he did salute the quarterdeck would not that have shown he had been respectful to the quarterdeck and everybody on it?'

'No. Not in the way he came over. No.'

'Do you expect the Admiral every time he comes over the side to answer the salute of every senior officer who happens to be there, individually?'

'I have been in flagships for a large portion of my service and that has always been what I have seen.'

Daniel was asked if he thought that every possible assistance and seamanlike facility had been given to the Admiral when he came alongside *Royal Oak* in his barge. He said it had and that no boat rope had been lowered because the arrangement had been for the barge to go straight to the derrick and be hoisted inboard with the Admiral's gear. Did he not consider it a seamanlike procedure to lower a boat rope when an Admiral's barge came alongside in an open anchorage?

Daniel answered that if there was only one passenger he saw no actual necessity, but he agreed that no harm would have been done had a boat rope been lowered. But were there not two passengers? Daniel believed there were. Were there not also three tin cases, valuable ones at that?

There were, answered Daniel and all the more reason for the barge to be hoisted inboard before they were removed.

When he was asked if he considered if there was anything unusual or un-officerlike in an admiral, when he was half-way up the ladder as Collard had described himself, looking down and seeing his valet struggling single-handed with his gear, in shouting to the sideboys and the Corporal of the Gangway to go down and lend him a hand, Daniel gave the remarkable answer that he thought there was.

The Prosecutor returned to the letter that Daniel wrote to his Captain.

'Do you agree,' he asked, 'that the result of your including in your letter extraneous matters, outside the orders you had been given, led to very considerable delay in your reasons in writing being handed in?'

Daniel: 'Undoubtedly yes.'

'For a comparatively simple incident?'

'That is a matter of opinion.'

'Anyway, you were given orders sometime after 9.15 p.m. on the 5th of March, and they were eventually received in manuscript signed by you on Thursday, the 8th of March?'

'I won't swear to "signed" because I knew it was going to be typed.'

'Now, when you decided to include in your letter matters outside the scope of your orders, I presume you realized you were taking a serious step?'

'Yes, in the degree that any report to my Captain is serious.'

'And a report which contained criticism of a superior officer would be even more important and serious?'

'It would be if I made personal criticisms about my superior officer.'

'Did you consider that if your Captain forwarded your letter that the Admiral and yourself could not possibly both of you remain in the same ship? Did you expect the Admiral would be superseded?'

'I did not, sir.'

'Did you appreciate you would possibly be removed?'

'I did when I knew the Captain was forwarding the letter.'

'Paragraph 8 of your letter says: "In the course of subsequent inquiries as to what had led up to the Admiral's fury . . ." Do you consider that a respectable way of speaking of your Admiral?'

'I tried many phrases to indicate what the state of the Admiral was – anger, upset – I don't know how many, but I chose that word as being the most accurate description. A man can be very angry and can still be more angry by being furious.'

'I will read on: "I learned incidentally that he had told the Captain in a loud voice and heated manner, in the presence of seamen moreover, that he was fed up with the ship. My informant stated that he felt disgusted at what he considered was the insulting behaviour of the Admiral to the Captain, although he did not hear in detail the rest of the abuse." Who was your informant? Will you tell the court?'

'Must I, sir? He is a very junior officer.'

'I don't wish to press. This informant – a very junior officer – did not hear the details of any further abuse. Then how did your informant know there was any further abuse if he didn't hear it?'

'He heard a certain amount which I summarized, and he told me he heard angry voices and saw gesticulations, and the whole effect was to disgust him.'

'Do you think he was eavesdropping?'

'I think I should say quite impossible.'

'It is the custom of the Service, is it not, and I presume it is carried out in the *Royal Oak*, when senior officers are on deck talking, all junior officers clear off to the other side of the deck?'

'Yes, but if the row was a big one, it would have to be a very big deck.'

'You were there at the time?'

'Yes.'

'Did you hear anything?'

'No, I didn't.'

'Can you account for that?'

'Because I was very busy with the ladders. I had definite work to do and I expect I was making a good deal of noise myself.'

'What attempt did you make to corroborate your informant's story?'

'I made none. I felt the important thing was to let the Captain know that this was the rumour.'

'Paragraph 9 of your letter says this: "This concludes my report on the events, but I consider it my duty to point out what serious harm is done by such incidents. On the last occasion great pains were necessary to restore the respect of the Admiral in the public opinion of the wardroom and of the lower deck, and I feel confident that this has been achieved." The last of these, I presume, refers to January the twelfth? Why rake it up again?'

'Because of the remarks in the wardroom which had used the words "Another bust-up on the quarterdeck" and also the Captain had reserved the right of referring to this matter should a further incident occur, and I had no doubt it was in everybody's mind. The whole thing surged up again.'

'Do you agree that any reservations the Captain made were no business of yours?'

'I don't think I do. I consider it is my job as Commander to understand my Captain's reservations.'

'And you raked it up on your own, did you?'

It was less than twenty-four hours since Captain Calvert, the amateur prosecutor, had been chided by the court for asking nothing but a succession of leading questions. Clearly he had spent the night in study and research. His cross-examination already had Daniel bothered. Now he was to strike deeper. He asked the witness to explain why he had written that the discipline and morale of the ship were grievously affected. In answer Daniel had to admit that he had only the Chaplain's word for this. He said that when he first joined the ship he had instructed the Chaplain to listen to lower deck conversations and to report their general mood. At the same time, he had pledged his word that he would not press the Chaplain for names or any other details that would put the man of being in the position of a tale carrier.

Daniel said he had other sources to sound out morale in *Royal Oak*, but in cross-examination, and pressed over and over again, he had to confess he had never used them – not the Master at Arms; not the Royal Marine Sergeant Major; not the Chief Stoker.

The Prosecutor: 'Yet you felt justified in writing: "This . . . has had a very serious effect on discipline and morale"?'

'That was my honest opinion.'

'And this authority, I understand, was the Chaplain and no one else?'

'I questioned certain lieutenant-commanders. I also questioned . . .'

'Excuse me, am I right in saying you questioned them after you had written the letter?'

'Yes, I consulted no one before I wrote it.'

The cross-examiner brought up the matter of the reading of Dewar's letter to the wardroom just before the court of inquiry. Daniel was in for another rough ride. Yes, he admitted, he did know that the Captain's letter had been marked 'Secret'. No, he had not had the Captain's permission to read it, but he could not think of any other way of finding officers who could give evidence on the various points raised in the letter. No, he did not agree that it would have been quite sufficient and very simple to ask officers to give evidence for or against incidents that had happened on 12 January, the night of the dance, on 5 March, when the Admiral landed, and on 6 March, when he had returned on board. Yes, there were quite a number of junior officers present and he did consider it in the best interests of discipline and of the Navy that they should hear the Captain's letter being read out.

Why, if he was not certain which officers could give evidence, did he not send them all along to the inquiry so that the court could decide? Because it was contrary to the Captain's wishes. No, the Captain would not have placed him under arrest if he had taken along all the officers.

The Prosecutor: 'I must refer you to your own letter once again. Paragraph 10: "Apologies would serve no useful purpose, but assurance is urgently necessary that discipline, which must depend upon respect for rank, will not be undermined in this way". Do you suggest you were living up to that axiom by reading your Captain's letter to this assembly of officers?'

'I do, sir.'

'Do you realize, once this letter had been read out to the assembly of officers, the question of its being secret had passed beyond all bounds of control?'

'I do not consider that is true sir. As far as I know the officers of the ship have been extremely loyal in not talking about the contents of that letter. The incidents given in the letter were freely discussed. I gave them no news they didn't know.

Kimball re-examined his witness for a few moments without taking matters any further forward or, for that matter, strengthening Daniel's case. Then the court itself took a hand. The President asked a simple question that had Daniel floundering. When the Admiral had boarded *Royal Oak* from his barge that afternoon in March was he wearing plain clothes or was he in uniform?

Daniel answered, 'I can't swear to it. I think he was in uniform.'

The President echoed his answer, 'You can't swear to it?'

Daniel's reply was, 'No, I can't absolutely swear to it.'

It would be hard to think of a more astounding answer from a naval officer who had just given evidence against his Admiral for humiliating his Captain in front of the ship's company by not saluting. For if Collard were wearing plain clothes it would have been quite impossible for him to salute.

True, he could have raised his civilian hat politely – and no naval officer ever went bare-headed – but the court did not explore this possibility. In its view, enough time had been wasted already.

II

'A Devil of a Row Aft'

Daniel had been giving evidence for nearly five hours. Now it was Captain Dewar's turn. White-gloved and wearing his sword – it was not time yet for *him* to surrender it to the court – he took his place before the long table.

Fortunately for authority, now extremely anxious to get the trials out of the way, his evidence was comparatively brief. He gave his version of Collard's behaviour at the dance and said that the Admiral became so excited at one stage that he had to suggest to him that it was neither the time nor the place to have a discussion and, in an attempt to cut Collard short, he edged away. In the Admiral's day cabin afterwards, he had said to Collard, 'I want to talk to you about threatening me on the quarterdeck last night in the presence of guests.'

Dewar was not allowed to continue his description of the interview because the Deputy Judge Advocate objected that Daniel had not been present.

He went on to confirm Daniel's story of the discussion in the cabin when all three had been together. He added that Collard swore on his honour that he had never used the word 'bugger'.

Dewar said that when Daniel was first appointed to the ship he was told that his most important duty was to keep in touch with the petty officers and master at arms and other subordinates so that he could give his captain an accurate picture of the discipline and state of the ship. He added that Daniel's methods had a very great effect on *Royal Oak*. When he had first arrived the ship was outwardly efficient, but, in the Captain's opinion, and in some ways, she was a dead ship. Daniel had entirely altered the situation in a couple of months. The men became much happier and the officers keener and the ship generally more efficient.

In cross-examination he replied that he thought Daniel's letter was entirely in accordance with his orders. He did not agree that it criticized the Admiral. Instead, it remarked on the effect of the Admiral's conduct on the ship. He did not think that Daniel's phrase 'in anticipation of vindictive fault-finding' was a criticism of the Admiral. It was an attempt to show the effect of his conduct. He thought that the dance incident would have badly affected morale and discipline if Daniel had not acted as he had.

The Prosecutor: 'Were you yourself apprehensive about the forthcoming inspection of the ship by the Admiral?'

Dewar: 'I really did not think much about it. If I had I should not have been apprehensive. I should have expected, in view of these incidents, one might get rather a rough time.'

In further cross-examination, Dewar said that Collard had been wearing uniform when he came aboard *Royal Oak* from his barge. He had not saluted the quarterdeck.

Daniel had not been appointed to the ship by the Admiralty but at the request of Collard and Dewar. Collard had applied at Dewar's request.

The next witness was No. RMB 1413 Bandmaster First Class Percy Edward Barnacle. He stated that on the night of the dance the band had played one tune which had received an encore and the band had just played it again and the applause died down when the Admiral beckoned to him with his finger and at the same time approached the bandstand. The Admiral said, 'Come here, you bugger. Call yourself a flagship's bandmaster?' Then he added, 'I will have you sent home. I have never heard such a bloody noise in all my life. Can't you play dance music? In any case I will report you. Now go and see if you can do better.'

Barnacle: 'I replied to the Admiral, "I will do my very best sir".' That interruption, added the Bandmaster, caused a slight delay in the programme.

The band played one more number, then Barnacle took them below. The instruments were taken to the band room and there two or three bandsmen asked Barnacle if it was in order for them to put in a request to leave the ship. At this point the Deputy Judge Advocate stopped the Bandmaster from giving any more hearsay evidence.

Then came the question that Barnacle had been dreading. Kimball paused, looked at him hard and then asked, 'In your opinion, how was the band playing that evening?'

The Bandmaster waited even longer before, and, still stiffly at attention, he gave the well-rehearsed answer: 'Just as well as usual, Sir.' He had obviously tucked any thoughts of his alcoholic cornettist well into the back of his mind.

To Barnacle's relief, the subject was changed. He told the court that sometime later he was taken before Commander Daniel who said that the Admiral had offered an apology through him.

The Deputy Judge Advocate intervened: 'Did you make any request to your superior officer the morning following the dance, in regard to this incident? If so, what were the terms of this request?'

Barnacle: 'The terms of the request were that I requested to leave the Service.'

Then the President followed the line of questioning. 'Why,' he asked, 'did you want to leave the Service?'

The Bandmaster replied, 'In view of my past recommendations from flag officers. The situation was that I was distracted by being spoken to in such a manner.'

Light comedy arrived with the next witness, No. RMB 1445 Musician Walter Guerin, who played the cornet in *Royal Oak*'s band. He contradicted his Bandmaster by saying that they had played two encores to a dance just before the Admiral approached. The Admiral beckoned to Barnacle and Guerin heard him say, 'Come here you, come here you, you bugger,' and pointed to the deck before him.

It was not the evidence that suddenly had the nine senior officers of the court laughing uncontrollably but Guerin's masterly imitation of Collard's voice and manner. It took quite a while for that hangar aboard HMS *Eagle* to come to order and resume its solemnity.

Commander Malby Brownlow was then called. He was navigation commander of *Royal Oak* and, being the senior commander on board, was also president of the wardroom mess. In that latter capacity, he said, he was responsible for the conduct and behaviour of the officers in that mess and consequently felt it necessary to know what was going on. He had been ashore on the night of the dance but Daniel came to him later with his letter and asked if the facts he had stated with regard to the feelings of the wardroom were correct.

Brownlow told the court, 'I felt very strongly that the whole world ought to know that we resented the incident which had taken place on board.'

The Prosecutor: 'Do you really believe it to be in the interests of the Service that the whole world should be told of this affair?'

Brownlow hesitated for quite a while before he answered, 'Yes'.

'You still hold that opinion today?'

'Yes. Certainly.'

Brownlow was followed by *Royal Oak*'s first lieutenant and gunnery officer, Lieutenant-Commander George O'Donnell. He gave evidence that, very soon after Daniel had been appointed to the ship, he sent for the First Lieutenant to his cabin and gave an order that he was to be kept informed of the opinions of the lower deck and wardroom in matters affecting the morale of the crew. Daniel added that anything said in his cabin would go no further and that if he did not want to hear what O'Donnell had to tell him he would stop him. Soon after that O'Donnell did have occasion to put these instructions into effect. On the Saturday after the dance he sought out Daniel in his cabin. It was about nine o'clock in the evening. O'Donnell said to the Commander, 'I would like to see you privately, sir. The matter I want to see you about is concerning the incident of the dance on Thursday night. I think you should know that the whole matter of the incident that occurred is being discussed in Malta. When I got home last night my wife told me.'

Daniel's answer was that they must do their best to stop the rumours. He said he relied on O'Donnell, as First Lieutenant, to stop wardroom chatter. O'Donnell had replied that he could not be responsible for dealing with the three-stripers in the mess for they were so indignant about the events at the dance that he was certain they would not listen to him, but he would do all he possibly could with officers junior to him.

On 5 March – the day the Admiral went ashore in his barge – there had been trouble on the fo'c'sle with a jammed cable. When it was cleared O'Donnell went down to the wardroom to report the fact. As he entered the anteroom he heard someone among a group of officers say, 'There was a devil of a row aft'.

A few days later he was asked to go to Daniel's cabin. Two other lieutenant-commanders were already there. Daniel told him to shut the door and then said he had sent for the ship's lieutenant-commanders as he thought that they represented the opinion of the wardroom better than anyone else. Then Daniel announced very seriously indeed, 'I have committed myself,' and proceeded to read out extracts from a typewritten sheet on the desk before him. O'Donnell remembered phrases such as: 'Among wardroom officers, those who had the mortifying experience of witnessing these scenes are inflamed with anger and deeply resentful of the humiliation . . .' and 'My recent appeal to look forward to the inspection, thereby making it serve a useful purpose for the efficiency of the Service, has been reversed by the anticipation of vindictive fault-finding'.

Daniel then begged the three officers, 'If I have in any case overstated the case, for God's sake stop me.'

The three lieutenant-commanders reflected and then assured him that he had not.

O'Donnell told the court that he still thought the letter was a fair representation of the wardroom's feelings.

When the Prosecutor got to his feet and started his cross-examination he soon found himself wallowing in technicalities about jammed anchor cables. Both Prosecutor and witness were happily involved in discussing probable causes and explanations for the jamming when the impatient court put a stop to things and declared that it would have no more questions along those lines.

In further cross-examination O'Donnell said that by 6 March – the day the Admiral returned on board – he had given up attempting to stop wardroom chatter. He heard it among senior officers as well as juniors, but he took no notice. Apart from that he had no time to check such conversations.

Prosecutor: 'You had time to listen to it but not to check it?'

'I heard it but I did not say I listened to it.'

The questioning turned to the day of the court of inquiry and the occasion when Daniel had started to read out the Captain's letter to the wardroom officers. In his answers O'Donnell stoutly denied that he was disgusted at such behaviour. Nor was he taken aback. He had even read out part of it himself while the Commander was sent for by Dewar. He disagreed that it was not fit hearing for the junior officers present. In his view it was the only way to collect witnesses.

Lieutenant-Commander Archie Murray, the second senior lieutenant-commander aboard *Royal Oak*, was sworn in. Technically he was Daniel's assistant. He described what he called the intense indignation in the wardroom on the Friday and Saturday following the dance. He had also been in charge of the main derrick on the occasion when the Rear-Admiral returned in his barge. His orders from Daniel were to hoist that barge inboard once Collard had quitted it. It was here that Kimball, who was examining him, either pressed too hard or showed his lack of knowledge of the subject.

109

'What do you say,' he asked, 'as to the suitability of weather conditions for hoisting the barge inboard on that occasion?' Murray answered bluntly, 'I would have preferred not to.'

In an effort to retrieve the situation and to remove any suspicion that Collard's mood that day had some justification, Kimball went on to ask, 'Could it have been done?' Murray answered that it could.

By the time another witness had been heard it was seven o'clock and the end of another long day in the carrier's hangar. All idea that the trials would be swiftly dealt with and the pleasant prospects of a quick start to the Spring cruise had disappeared. After two days Daniel's case was not even over and there was still more evidence to come.

Strong evidence it was too. Promptly at nine-thirty the next morning Major Claude Attwood strode forward to give evidence. From the night of the dance he had been an angry critic of the Rear-Admiral and his behaviour. Nothing was going to persuade him that Collard's action had not been a grave slur on the Royal Marines that he commanded aboard *Royal Oak*.

He told the court that on the day of the dance he had been in camp ashore with a machine-gun party. He had returned to the ship especially for the dance. During the evening he had heard an angry voice and had seen Collard shaking his hand at the band and talking loudly. Attwood said he had wanted to intervene then but his dancing partner had checked him. There was no question of it being a trifling, unnoticed incident. According to Attwood everyone was standing around and watching. There were a large number of people and they were all staring.

After the dance he had returned to the camp ashore and did not rejoin *Royal Oak* until about noon two days later. Immediately he set foot on board his second-in-command met him on the quarterdeck and told him that Bandmaster Barnacle had asked to be relieved from the band. Had Barnacle's original request gone through, he would have forfeited seventeen pensionable years' service. Attwood smartly sought out Daniel and told him he wished to protest against what he considered to be a reflection on his Corps and himself.

'I made it pretty clear to him,' Attwood told the court, 'that I felt very indignant about it.'

As far as he was concerned he was prepared to leave things in the Captain's hands and, should any further action take place, he was prepared to support it. Later Daniel told him the Admiral had apologized. Attwood said he was prepared to accept this but only on the condition that if any other incident concerning Collard occurred, then he would bring the matter up again. Daniel said that the Admiral would be having a drink in the wardroom. Attwood added that he attended just to be in at the closing of the incident. After Collard had left, Attwood heard Daniel say that no further reference was to be made to the events at the dance. But shortly afterwards, while he was having a wardroom drink with Daniel and another officer, Attwood said he made a comment about the Admiral. Daniel promptly left them, went to the quarterdeck and sent for the Major and warned him about making such remarks.

Kimball: 'Was that a casual or formal conversation?'

Attwood: 'Distinctly formal.'

The Major went on to tell the court that he agreed with the phrase in Daniel's letter stating: 'Among wardroom officers, those who had the mortifying experience of witnessing these scenes are inflamed with indignation and all officers are deeply resentful.' It was a fair description of the attitude of the wardroom. There seemed to be a certain amount of feeling that if something were not done, then there would be trouble in the ship.

Attwood added, 'I myself heard remarks such as: "What is the good of doing anything. The Admiral is never pleased".'

After the departure of the stubborn and indignant Major, the court had, at last, arrived at the closing speeches.

They made a most dissimilar pair, Day Kimball, in his black jacket and pinstriped trousers, forever hitching up the shoulders of his gown, appearing for the defence, and Captain Thomas Calvert, DSO, for the prosecution, in his frock coat, sword belt, braid and medals – Kimball with his East Coast American accent; Calvert's, in contrast, as English as a public school and the navy could make it. Yet both found themselves united in arguing intensely over the rights and wrongs of a matter that, in its origins, would hardly amount to much more than a ripple at a golf club dance. But now senior officers' careers were at stake.

Put briefly and simply – but alas, to the chagrin of the nine members of the court, weary in their seats, Kimball was neither brief nor simple – the defence was as follows.

In answer to the first two charges, Daniel had no idea, when he was ordered by the Captain to explain the reasons for the Admiral's dissatisfaction with the arrangements for the accommodation ladder, that it would ever go beyond the Captain. And if, while writing his letter, he had expressed his concern about the Admiral's effect upon the ship's morale and discipline, to whom else could the officer most concerned on such subjects write, save to his own Captain?

When Daniel realized that his letter was being sent forward to the Admiral, he had at least made the effort of checking with the more senior officers in the wardroom that it was justified.

As for the third and fourth charges, Daniel had no option but to read any letter of complaint aloud to junior officers in the wardroom, given the extremely brief time he had to secure witnesses for the court of inquiry.

Kimball agreed that in one respect the incidents leading to the court martial were farcical; never had there been a storm in a tinier teacup. But for his client the outcome was grave – for the Royal Navy too. If Daniel were found guilty, then any officer would be convinced that any complaint he made, however justified, could only result in punishment for himself.

Calvert was shorter, much shorter. He argued thus. When Daniel realized his letter was to be forwarded to the Admiral, with all its insubordinate remarks, he had ample time to withdraw it. Instead he consulted other officers and then made sure it went forward. Daniel's argument was that he had written it for the good of the ship and her morale and discipline. But apart from a few third-hand wardroom remarks the defence had produced no evidence at all that *Royal Oak* was in any way an unhappy ship.

As for reading the letters aloud in the wardroom in order to secure witnesses, surely some simple, unsubversive way could easily have been found. Merely detailing officers who had been present at the various incidents would have been enough. There was no shadow of doubt in Calvert's mind that Commander Daniel was guilty on all four charges.

There was a sudden clamour of warning bells high up on the bulkhead of the hangar; the great armour-plated doors slowly started to creep shut as witnesses, lawyers, spectators and pressmen were herded away beyond them. The court was about to decide on its verdict.

Half an hour elapsed before those steel doors were reopened. Daniel marched in, escorted by his guardian officer. Behind them filed an anticipatory audience. Daniel had to approach the baize-covered table from an angle. As he neared it he turned his head anxiously to his left in order to catch a glimpse of his unsheathed sword. Its point was towards him. It told him all he needed to know. He had been found guilty on at least one charge. It turned out to be very much worse than that!

The Deputy Judge Advocate rose to his feet and announced that all the charges against the accused had been proved. He held a single sheet of hand-written paper. It bore the signatures of the nine members of the board. They were all in unison.

Proceedings then took on a form familiar in any civilian court. Daniel was to be given the opportunity to plead in mitigation of the sentence that was surely coming. He was asked if he wished to hand in his certificates – those vital documents recording a naval officer's career and his various superiors' comments. Because of his long service, the accused was able to produce a considerable sheaf. One by one they were solemnly read out, right from the time, twenty-three years before, when he was serving as a midshipman in HMS *Bulwark*. His captain's report on him then was that he had served with sobriety, zeal and attention and ended, 'This officer's abilities are of a very high order'. According to *The Times* the list went on to sound like an illustrious roll call: *Lord Nelson, Isis, Albion, Duncan, Calliope, Royalist, Dauntless, Valiant* and *Barham*. All the reports were highly favourable, including one from a vice-admiral. At least two of them spoke of his tact in dealing with other officers.

Strangely, one comment made twelve years earlier when he was serving as a lieutenant in *Vivid I* for a brief few weeks was signed by Dewar as his commanding officer. It declared that Daniel was a zealous gunnery officer.

The prosecution told the court that it could not produce any evidence that Daniel had ever been censured before and stated that he had never been court-martialled. Daniel was asked if he wished to address the court in mitigation of his offence or call any character witnesses. He declined.

The bulkhead bells clattered again, the hangar was cleared and the court was left to decide Daniel's punishment. When the trial reopened all the witnesses lined up formally behind the President and faced Daniel. Only Rear-Admiral Collard had chosen to be absent. The sentence was stern. Daniel was to be dismissed his ship and severely reprimanded. The only worse penalty he could have incurred would to have been dismissed the Service. But the practical results were very much the same. At a time when the Navy was economizing and saving every penny it could, there would be little room for a commander with such a blot on his record.

Incidentally, the ship from which Daniel was formally dismissed was HMS *Cormorant*, a small and ancient sloop now lending her name to the headquarters of the Rear-Admiral-in-Charge, Gibraltar. A naval officer could never be without his ship even if it was something of a charade. So when Collard and his two subordinates had been removed from *Royal Oak*, they had found themselves borne on *Cormorant*'s books.

As Daniel and his small party made their disconsolate way ashore and to their hotel, another naval occasion was also ending in something much like disaster on that very same day.

The Atlantic Fleet had left Gibraltar in a hurry to be reviewed at Portland by King Amanullah of Afghanistan. The morning had dawned grey and overcast. A few hours later heavy and ceaseless rain swept across the harbour. Outside more than half a gale was blowing. Still the Atlantic Fleet put to sea before noon and was soon joined by the royal barge rolling and pitching in the broken waves. The King of Afghanistan, accompanied by the Duke of York, later to be King George VI, carefully mounted the heaving accommodation ladder of the fleet flagship, HMS *Nelson* – the Queen of Afghanistan and her court had, at the last moment, excused themselves from the review – and was saluted by a Royal Marine band playing his national anthem, his blood-red royal standard streaming out at the masthead. How much King Amanullah heard of the music in the buffetting wind is hard to say, but he was certainly much more civil than Rear-Admiral Collard was when that admiral heard his band play.

Huddled in his greatcoat, he was led aloft to a special viewing platform high above *Nelson*'s conning tower. By now the weather had thickened and visibility deteriorated so the first event on the well-rehearsed programme, an attack by submarines on *Nelson*, had to be abandoned. Instead four destroyers, steaming as fast as they dare, under the conditions and already shipping green water over their upper decks, attempted a depth-charge attack. Watching their plight, *Nelson* obligingly changed on to a more accommodating course. Even so the thunder of the explosions was hardly heard above the weather.

The sky was darkening all the time and when the Fleet steamed past *Nelson*, firing a twenty-one gun salute as they went, they could hardly be seen. Somewhere overhead a flying boat had managed to locate the flagship and circled in homage. This was the only aircraft seen that day. A mock attack on *Nelson* by the carrier *Furious* had to be cancelled as did the set piece of the day, the full-blooded target shooting of all the Fleet's big guns.

At around six o'clock that evening the salt-stained, sea-streaming Atlantic Fleet returned King Amanullah to the shelter of Spithead to put him aboard the Southern Railway's ferry paddle steamer *Duchess of Fife*, also proudly wearing the Royal Afghan ensign. She chugged away to the sound of that Marine band, once again playing Amanullah's national anthem.

The King sent a message expressing his satisfaction, though whether it was at the Navy's hospitality or at the thought of approaching dry land again, it is hard to say. It was probably, and entirely, coincidental that a few days later His Majesty entered a Berlin nursing home for an operation on his tonsils.

There must have been much to talk about in the wardrooms of the Atlantic Fleet that stormy night. There would have been even more had communications made it possible for them to know the fate of a dispirited commander out in Gibraltar.

12

'Deliberate Disloyalty?'

A NEW PANEL OF JUDGES had to be selected for Captain Dewar's court martial. There was the matter of superiority for one thing. Being of higher rank than Daniel and, by regulation, having to be tried by his seniors and peers, five rear-admirals and four captains were chosen to sit in judgement.

The court assembled aboard HMS *Eagle* on the morning of 4 April. There was no sign of the Mediterranean spring; it was yet another chill, grey and overcast day. Dewar, swordless as was the custom, was escorted before his judges. Then the audience was admitted. It was very much the same mixture as before; curious naval officers, reporters, a sprinkling of civilians and Mrs Dewar supported by the unhappy Mrs Daniel. The traditional question was asked. Had either the defence or the prosecution any objection to any member of the court. The monocled Prosecutor, Rear-Admiral William Boyle, CB, Commander of the First Cruiser Squadron, had.

Showing great fairness, he argued against the presence of Rear-Admiral The Hon Herbert Meade, CB, CVO, DSO, on the grounds that he had been a member of the original court of inquiry, and of Rear-Admiral Wilfred Tomkinson because, as Chief of Staff to Sir Roger Keyes, he had read the minutes of the inquiry.

The court so recently assembled was immediately cleared of spectators and the two officers next in seniority, Captain Hubert Monroe, DSO, of the battleship *Ramillies* and Captain Arthur Bedford of the flagship *Queen Elizabeth*, were substituted for the controversial admirals.

Then the Prosecutor raised another objection, this time to Collard himself. According to the rules, Collard was eligible to become a substitute member of the court should the need arise, say in case of sickness. The Rear-Admiral Prosecutor pointed out emphatically that Collard was already a witness for the prosecution. This protest, too, was allowed.

When it was Dewar's turn, he made no objection for there was no need. His work had been done for him.

Day Kimball was also in court. He was supposed to assist Dewar but the Captain had very definite ideas of his own as to how his case should be conducted and he was going to brook little interference from the civilian in striped trousers.

The two charges against Dewar were that, being a person subject to the Naval Discipline Act, he was guilty of an act to the prejudice of good order and naval discipline in that he accepted and forwarded a letter addressed to him by Daniel, the terms of which were subversive of discipline. And that he did the same thing with a letter that, contrary to King's Regulations and Admiralty Instructions, Article 11, contained remarks and criticism on the conduct or orders of his superior officer, Rear-Admiral Bernard St George Collard.

Quietly Dewar pleaded 'Not Guilty' to both accusations.

The first witness called for the prosecution was Dewar's secretary aboard *Royal Oak*, Paymaster Lieutenant Crichton. He gave evidence as to his role in typing the letters of Dewar and Daniel. When he finished, Dewar took over the cross-examination himself, leaving Kimball to sit silent.

Dewar: 'Were you my secretary?'

Crichton: 'Yes.'

Dewar: 'In the course of your duties you had seen me on a great many different occasions?'

Crichton: 'Many.'

Dewar: 'From your observation do you think I am the sort of person to lose my temper with an admiral?'

Crichton: 'Never.'

The witness agreed that Dewar had stressed the need for secrecy in the typing of the letters, and that the wardroom was indignant about the incidents that had occurred on board. He also stated that he was well aware of the forthcoming inspection of *Royal Oak* by Collard.

Dewar: 'When you heard of the incidents described in my letter and you saw that the Captain and the Admiral were evidently at loggerheads, did it ever enter your head that the result of the inspection might be slightly prejudiced?'

Crichton: 'Yes.'

Rear-Admiral Collard was the next witness. The atmosphere in *Eagle*'s chill steel hangar, its canvas awnings buffetted by a squall of rain from time to time, sensibly heightened. There was a distinct tension in the air, almost as though a famous criminal lawyer was about to cross-examine the accused in some sensational trial at the Old Bailey. For the first time since both men had so abruptly quitted *Royal Oak*, Collard and Dewar were about to come face to face – the Rear-Admiral with a temper of quicksilver and the quiet, intellectually-minded Captain determined to clear his name.

But the drama would have to wait until the Vice-Admiral Prosecutor had his turn with the witness. For the second time inside a week Collard stood before the long, baize-covered table. He was as immaculate and as pinkly shaven as ever and radiated an air of utter impartiality and lack of involvement, almost like the perfect policeman giving evidence, telling the facts and letting the fault and blame lay where they fell.

Nor in any way was his attitude a pretence. Collard's emotions were always an open book, to be read in his face with no difficulty at all. Now he gave the air that if it were not for the trifling matter of his having to give evidence and the earlier objection to his presence by the prosecution, he might well have been sitting in impartial judgement at that table with his fellow rear-admirals. He gave no hint whatsoever that, although he had not been accused himself, he was as much on trial as his two subordinate officers. While everyone else might gossip and marvel at a newly appointed rear-admiral who had lost his flag ship so quickly, there was no reading any such thought in Collard's attitude as he turned his bright eyes to the Prosecutor.

The first few questions alone would have disconcerted many another man. So would the answers that he was forced to give. Yes, he had been Rear-Admiral, First Battle Squadron recently. Yes, he had taken up that appointment on Monday, 7 November, 1927. Yes, he had struck his flag on Monday, 12 March, 1928. But it took only the sixth question for Collard to lose his dispassion and give a flash of that temper he had shown during Daniel's trial. He was asked how Dewar came to be appointed as his flag captain and chief staff officer.

'I was asked by the First Lord of the Admiralty if I had any objection to Captain Dewar being appointed as my Flag Captain. I replied that I had no objection.' He was about to say more when the Deputy Judge Advocate objected on the grounds that the answer was hearsay.

The questioning continued. No, Collard had not known Dewar before. He had met him, at the most, only once or twice in his life. His relations with him as staff officer were correct but not intimate in any way. Collard said he found it impossible to make friends with his staff captain, however hard he tried. The attitude between them was perfectly correct from a Service point of view but there was no friendship.

By now it was becoming apparent to the court and the spectators how strongly Collard stressed the word '*my*' when he referred to his Flag Captain, just as it had when he had given evidence during Commander Daniel's trial.

The Prosecutor: 'Did you place implicit confidence in him?'

Collard: 'No. I cannot say I did.'

He was handed the letters written by Dewar and Daniel and asked if he had seen them before. Collard answered, 'I have. At about 1400 hours on Friday, the ninth of March, I was in my cabin with my secretary doing some paperwork. The Flag Captain came in carrying a large buff envelope which he placed down on the right-hand side of my table, with the remark "Complaints for the Vice-Admiral". He then left my cabin.'

Collard was asked to comment on the letters from a disciplinary point of view, but Dewar got to his feet and objected, pointing out with considerable truth that that was what the court was there to decide.

Soon afterwards the Prosecutor concluded his examination.

Dewar rose to his feet to cross-examine and everyone in that hangar sat up more sharply. The Rear-Admiral and the Captain were about to have matters out for the first time in public.

Collard seemed utterly composed. If he had not been so service-like, so square-shouldered and immaculately erect, then it would have been easy to compare him with a sun-drowsing lizard ready to flick out a tongue at a passing fly, but hardly bothered whether any such creature should pass his sleepy horizon at all.

On the other hand Dewar was a distinguished graduate of the Royal Navy Staff Course where, above all, officers were measured by their ability to express their thoughts with sharp clarity, to marshal their ideas in crisp and impeccable order. Yet all this training seemed to have deserted him as he stood up and asked Collard his first question. It was so convoluted, so orotund, as to be incomprehensible.

The Prosecutor adjusted his eyeglass and protested. Rear-Admiral

Townsend, the President of the court, growled that the court wanted plain questions and no trimmings. It was not a good start for the accused Captain.

What he had been trying to ask was whether Collard agreed that the reason that, as Captain, he had send on Daniel's letter largely depended on the truth or otherwise of the incidents described in his own letter. Once he had grasped the question, Collard answered stoutly that he did not agree.

Dewar attacked from another angle. He asked Collard, 'Will you give me your version of the incident described in paragraph two which I will read to you: "At an evening dance given on board HMS *Royal Oak* on 12 January, Rear-Admiral Collard threatened me, in the hearing of several guests, that if I did not make the Commander do his duty in introducing people to each other, he would make me rue it".'

Again the prosecution objected. How could all this be relevant?

Dewar was forced to plead to the court. He submitted that the justification for forwarding Daniel's letter very largely depended on the truth or falsehood of the report of the incidents in his own covering letter. The effect on his own career, if those incidents were not true, would most certainly be prejudicial.

Then Dewar played a trump card. He said that the point had arisen before he had left England on his way to the court martial. The legal branch of the Admiralty had doubted whether investigation of the incidents would be relevant to the two charges against him.

'I therefore wrote to the Admiralty,' Dewar told the court, 'and explained that, if this were so, I would have no chance with them of employment again, and I received a reply from Their Lordships, the last paragraph of which was to the effect that Their Lordships' sole purpose in sending Rear-Admiral Collard out here for cross-examination was so that the defence will have an opportunity of elucidating such facts as they may have to answer.'

Dewar asked the court if he might submit the letter and have it read out so that it could be relied on for whatever the defence regarded as relevant questions. Once more the court was cleared.

When everyone was called back the President pronounced, though he never explained why, that the Admiralty letter was not to be read out. However, the court would have no further objection to questions referring to incidents contained in the letters but that there was to be no hearsay evidence.

10 Mr C. Day Kimball, Commander Daniel and Captain Dewar about to board the liner *Malwa* on their way to Gibraltar and their courts martial. (see p.77)

11 Aboard HMS *Eagle*. (1) Captain Burges Watson, President. (2) Paymaster Captain Measham, Deputy Judge Advocate. (3) Captain Calvert, Prosecutor. (4) Commander Daniel. (5) Mr C. Day Kimball for the Defence and briefed by Mr Carrara. (6) On the left is the Provost Marshal. (7) Seated round the hangar are officers of the Fleet. Above them is the makeshift Press gallery. (*Daily Mail*).

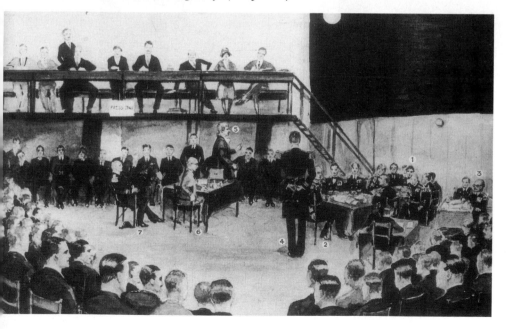

12–14 Arriving at HMS *Eagle* for the courts martial.
   Right: Rear-Admiral Collard.
   Below Left: Captain Dewar.
   Below Right: Commander Daniel.

'Is that clear?' barked the President, who, as Admiral Superintendent of Gibraltar, was reputed to have a testy side to his nature.

Dewar, having finally overcome the court's reluctance to discuss Collard's behaviour, gently agreed and returned to his battle with his Rear-Admiral, who, while the argument had been going on, had assumed an air of amused indifference.

Once again Collard asked him about the dance and whether Collard had said Daniel was not doing his duty. Presenting the air of a man who was determined to be patient and even long-suffering if need be, the witness answered at some length. In the course of it he said that when he had arrived on the quarterdeck with his guests, after his own private dinner, he was immediately struck by the number of ladies sitting out without partners. He had approached Dewar who had answered that it would be all right presently when the dance really got going. Collard said he described the situation as a disgrace. Dewar had got very angry and retorted that it was the Commander's job. Collard had answered by saying that if Dewar could not make the Commander attend to his duties, then he would.

'That,' said the Rear-Admiral in a firm and dismissive voice, 'is all about that particular incident.'

For some reason known only to himself, and to the irritation of the court who manifestly felt that the less it heard about the dance the better, Dewar insisted in trying to pin Collard down as to which dance it was when this exchange took place.

The Rear-Admiral was not at a loss for a moment. He said sharply that he could not tell because the dance programme was unreadable. Dewar faced this new allegation by answering tartly, 'Thank you.'

Then he asked, 'Did you use the expression to me, "Bite the Commander"?'

Collard: 'As far as I remember I said to you, "If you cannot make the Commander do his job I will".'

Dewar: 'I asked you, did you use the expression "Bite the Commander"?'

Collard, still giving an impression of being at peace with the whole world, answered amiably, 'Not as far as I remember, but I should never have minded using it at all.'

No, he had not told Dewar at the time that he would make him rue it if the Commander did not do his duty, nor any words to that effect. No, he had not heard of people who thought that he had said any such thing. Yes, he would be surprised if there was a witness.

121

The questioning turned to Collard's attack on the Bandmaster. He had a full answer ready. Halfway through the dance, so he told the court, he thought that the band was playing perfectly abominable dance music. He heard complaints from guests all around him. He looked over at the band and saw that apparently the Bandmaster was taking no interest at all and his men looked sulky. At the end of that particular dance he had sought out the Commander, knowing that officer's considerable interest, and complained. He and Daniel had walked over to the bandstand and had stood three or four yards away so that the bandsmen could not hear and he had signalled Bandmaster Barnacle. True, he had told Barnacle that it was a bloody awful noise. Then he and Daniel had walked back to the ship's side where Daniel's partner was waiting, and, as they did so, had said, 'We cannot have a bloody man like that as the bandmaster of the flagship's band. He takes no interest in the band. Let us get rid of him.' Daniel had protested but Collard had insisted that the Royal Marines be sent below and the volunteer naval band produced.

There was not one mention in his answer of the word 'Bugger'. What is more, he denied using it when Dewar asked him.

Dewar: 'The words you said, were they not in the hearing of guests?'

Collard: 'It was in the view of all. I suppose there were a great many guests but the words I said were not in the hearing of anybody.'

'Would it not be in the hearing of the bandsmen?'

'I should say it was absolutely impossible for any of the bandsmen to have overheard the conversation.'

'Would you be surprised to hear that there are five bandsmen who are prepared to swear that they not only heard you but they heard the word "Bugger"?'

'I would.'

'Do you think they are lying?'

'I think so, not having heard their evidence.'

'Did you shake your fist at the Bandmaster?'

'I do not know.'

'Would you be surprised to hear that there is a witness who saw you?'

'I should.'

Dewar referred to the alleged row at the gangway when the dance was over while the guests were leaving. Collard answered flatly, and by now much less benevolently, 'So far as I know, you have entirely imagined that scene.'

After further objection by the court to the way in which Dewar was phrasing his questions and conducting his cross-examination, he turned to Daniel's letter and asked Collard if he thought it a fair statement that there was intense disgust and indignation among the wardroom officers at his behaviour. He got little change for his efforts. The Admiral answered, 'I have no means of knowing whether there was a great deal of discontent or intense disgust or indignation amongst the officers. Had there been so I suppose my Flag Captain would have informed me about it. As he did not I can only take it there was none.'

The Admiral had most certainly got his former Captain's range now. Every answering salvo became a hit.

Dewar: 'Do you think if this incident were true, the Bandmaster would likely be discouraged and dissatisfied by an incident of this kind?'

Collard: 'I really cannot answer for the Bandmaster.'

Dewar: 'Imagine yourself in the position of the Bandmaster on being taken out in front of your band and abused in this manner, would you have been discouraged or disheartened?'

Collard: 'I have no intention of imagining myself a bandmaster.'

Dewar: 'Do you think that this man asked to leave the Service after twenty years, and sacrifice his pension which he had accumulated, if he were not definitely discouraged or disheartened? Will you answer "Yes" or "No"?'

Collard: 'I will not. I will answer as I think fit. I do not know that he wanted to leave the Service.'

Dewar: 'Assuming that he did, may I have the answer "Yes" or "No"?'

Collard: 'Need I put myself in the Bandmaster's mind? Who is to know what is in the Bandmaster's mind?'

For this robust retort Collard almost earned himself a round of applause from the court. 'That is a very good answer,' declared the President.

Dewar: 'Are you acquainted with the last part of Article 11 of the King's Regulations and Admiralty Instructions, which is to the effect that if any officer go so far as to forget his duty as to discourage or make dissatisfied anyone with their work, any officers who shall witness such conduct shall at once report him to his captain?'

Collard: 'I think you have read it wrong.'

Dewar pressed on. In view of that particular Article, he asked Collard, did not the Admiral think it was his duty to report the incident of the dance band? Collard was not in the least put out. He gave it as his opinion that Dewar was entitled to make any report he felt it his duty to make. Then he added tartly, if the report were made in a proper manner.

At this stage, happy for Collard, most uncomfortable for Dewar, the court elected to rise for luncheon.

In the afternoon the duel between Admiral and Captain continued. They got round to Collard's interview with the Chaplain. Collard said that his Flag Lieutenant came to him sometime during the forenoon of 14 January and said, 'The Chaplain wishes to speak to you. Will you see him?' Collard continued, 'The Chaplain came in looking very ill at ease and said, "May I speak to you about a matter that is worrying me?" I said, "Yes. Go ahead." He said, "I have heard a rumour that you called the Bandmaster a bugger during the dance on Thursday night." I instantly and indignantly denied this and told the Chaplain he could contradict the rumour on my word of honour. The Chaplain said he would be very glad indeed to do so and that he would do so. He then left.'

Dewar: 'Did you threaten the Chaplain with a court martial?'

Collard: 'In the course of conversation with the Chaplain I pointed out that it was a very serious thing to do to come and accuse me on a false charge.'

Dewar: 'Did you say that specially severe sentences of imprisonment were given to those who brought false accusations against admirals?'

Collard: 'Not so far as I remember.'

At last Dewar was striking back. With those two answers that he had drawn from Collard, he had allowed the court a glimpse of the gallant Chaplain's ordeal in the Admiral's day cabin.

Later in his cross-examination Collard insisted that, after the Chaplain had called, he had wanted to see Bandmaster Barnacle himself but had been deterred by both Dewar and Commander Daniel, who had insisted that it would not be right and proper for an admiral to interview a bandmaster.

It was soon after this exchange that Collard's air of indifference, which had been evaporating for some time, finally went, and Dewar's sometime harassed attitude of polite austerity cracked. The two men came perilously close to the point of accusing each other of being downright liars.

Dewar: 'I put it to you that, after lunch, you asked me to come into your cabin and said, "I wish to squash a rumour that the Chaplain has brought me," and then I said to you, "First of all I wish to protest against your threat to me on Thursday night on the quarterdeck, in the presence of guests"?'

Collard: 'Nothing of the kind! I have described the conversation which took place, which is accurate.'

Dewar: 'Did you, at any period of this interview, say that this incident would mean a court martial for you?'

Collard: 'I did not.'

Dewar: 'When the Commander reported back to you, did you say, "Thank you, Commander, you have got me out of a damned nasty hole"?'

Collard: 'I did not. I congratulated the Commander on handling the business tactfully. I said I thought he had done well.'

The atmosphere in *Eagle*'s hangar and temporary court room became even more heated when the questioning turned to the occasion on which Admiral Collard had wished to leave *Royal Oak* in his barge. Collard said he left his cabin and arrived on deck to find nothing prepared. 'I turned round to the Flag Lieutenant,' he told the court, 'and said, "Did you give the messages to the Flag Captain and Commander about having the ladders ready?" He said, "Yes". I said, "Tell those two officers I wish to see them." The Commander came first and I said, "Why is not the ladder ready when I ordered it?" and he said he did not know. He would go and see about it. I said, "Go and see about it yourself," and he went. The Flag Captain came next, in an extremely bad temper, and said, "Did you send for me?" I said, "Yes I did. I ordered the ladders to be ready for me on arrival. I ordered my barge to come out by 9 o'clock and it is here, and I am on deck, and find nothing ready." I said, "I am sick of you as my Flag Captain, and either you will have to go or I shall ask permission to hoist my flag in another ship. I cannot get my orders carried out in this ship".'

Dewar: 'I put it to you, far from my being angry, I was extremely apprehensive and it was you who was extremely excited and angry?'

Collard: 'I consider that you were in an extremely bad temper.'

Dewar: 'When the Captain came aft you say you found fault with him. Are you sure it was not the ship you found fault with?'

Collard: 'Quite. Entirely my Flag Captain with whom I wished to find fault.'

Dewar: 'Did you not say you were fed up with the ship?'

Collard: 'I did not. I said I was fed up with my Flag Captain.'

Dewar: 'Would you be surprised if a witness was prepared to testify that he heard you say you were fed up with the ship?'

Collard: 'I should say that the witness did not hear what I did say, because we were standing by ourselves well aft on the port side.'

125

Dewar then asked a rather desperate question. Which side of a flag ship does the Admiral usually disembark? It got the answer it deserved as Collard growled irritatedly, 'On the side on which his barge is alongside.'

Dewar: 'Did you want another flag captain merely because your ladder was not ready?'

Collard: 'No I did not. There were many other reasons why I should have liked another flag captain.'

Dewar: 'I thought you said just now that your Service relations with your Flag Captain were perfectly correct?'

Collard: 'One wants more than perfectly correct Service relations with one's flag captain. One wants a loyal friend, one who will be one's right-hand man on every occasion. He will put his admiral's interests before everything else in the world.'

Dewar went on to ask: 'Even before the Service?'

Collard snorted in a loud voice, 'The admiral's interests are the interests of the Service.'

Then Dewar tried to inquire if the interests of the Service and the admiral were necessarily the same, but the court stopped him on the grounds that he had strayed far enough from the point already.

Dewar: 'Had you ever found fault with your Flag Captain before this alleged conversation?'

Collard: 'I had.'

Dewar: 'Will you state the occasion or occasions?'

Collard: 'On the 12th January at a dance given aboard the *Royal Oak*.'

Dewar: 'Was that the only occasion?'

Collard: 'The only serious occasion.'

Dewar: 'Will you tell me of any trivial occasion?'

Collard: 'No. I do not think there were any others. I was very forebearing sometimes.'

Dewar: 'Then it is correct to say that you told your Flag Captain that you were sick of him and wished to get rid of him on account of these two occasions?'

Collard: 'I did, because you do not come up in any way to what I require of my flag captain.'

Dewar: 'If I did not come up to your standard do you not think that you might have pointed out to me what was wrong on some previous occasion?'

Collard: 'My appointment was for one year and I thought we could go through that year without any break, providing there was a certain amount of give and take on each side.'

Dewar: 'Did you in the course of your conversation with me use the word "Midshipman"?'

Collard: 'Not so far as I remember; I think I said, "I consider I am treated abominably".'

The cross-examination moved on to the next day, 6 March, when the Admiral returned on board with his barge. Collard described how he looked down the accommodation ladder and saw his servant with the seas washing up to his knees, struggling with his luggage as it was being passed out of the barge. It was far too much for the man to handle by himself and the gear was in danger of going over the side. There was not an officer in sight.

Dewar: 'You say it was too rough to hoist in the barge. Will you admit that everything was ready for hoisting it in?'

Collard: 'I have not the least idea. That is not my business.'

Dewar: 'Do you think the Captain and Commander of the *Royal Oak* incapable of judging whether it is too rough to hoist a barge in?'

Collard: 'No. Quite capable I should say.'

Dewar: 'Had you advised the Captain that, as a general rule, boats should always be hoisted in before proceeding to sea?'

Collard: 'I had.'

Dewar: 'Had you intimated in advance that you did not want the barge hoisted in?'

Collard: 'I had not.'

Dewar: 'Would you agree that if the barge was going to be hoisted in, that it would be proper for your gear to be hoisted in with the barge?'

Collard: 'Certainly not.'

Dewar: 'Is it usual for an officer to stand at the top of the platform when an admiral comes over the side?'

Collard: 'I consider it would have been courteous to the admiral.'

Dewar: 'I mean actually on the platform?'

Collard: 'I certainly think that with a sea running and the admiral coming alongside, if I had been flag captain I should have been on that platform to see if I could help my admiral.'

Dewar: 'I put it to you that there was very little sea running?'

Collard: 'I should describe it as quite a heavy sea for a boat, which you would hardly perhaps appreciate from the security of the quarterdeck so well as I should appreciate it from my barge.'

Dewar: 'Can you tell me why you supervised the operation?'

Collard: 'Because no one else offered to and if I had not I am afraid my gear would now be at the bottom of the sea because my servant happens to be rather a small man.'

Dewar then harked back to the discussion he had had with his Admiral on the quarterdeck before he went ashore in his barge. 'Supposing,' he asked, 'that conversation was within hearing of ratings and supposing an exaggerated account went round the messdeck and it was said that the Admiral told the Captain that he was no more use than a bloody midshipman, do you think that would have been bad for discipline?'

Collard answered that he did not think it would have any effect on the discipline of a ship.

Dewar: 'Supposing this conversation went round the messdeck and wardroom, might not some of the officers and men possibly think that you might be just a little prejudiced against the ship as commanded by a captain you were sick of and wanted to get rid of?'

Collard: 'I consider they might have thought I was a little prejudiced against my flag captain and not against the ship.'

Dewar: 'If you were captain of a ship and your admiral told you that he was sick of you and wanted to get rid of you, and if you had been doing your best to make the ship an efficient unit, would you not be discouraged?'

Collard: 'No, I should not. I should go to my admiral and say, "I think I should like to go to another ship".'

Dewar: 'Do you agree that the maintenance of discipline largely depends upon carrying out such formalities as saluting?'

Collard: 'I do.'

Dewar: 'Supposing that you did return on board and not return my salute in the presence of about a hundred men, would you say that that was bad for discipline?'

'Most decidedly not. The discipline of a good ship does not depend on that sort of trivial rubbish – the omission or not of one salute to His Majesty's quarterdeck.'

After that somewhat startling answer, Dewar next attempted to seek his Admiral's definition of discipline. It was here that the court threw up its hands. Practically all day long its members had been treated to the unseemly sight of a rear-admiral and senior captain at each other's throat, Dewar intense and totally humourless – quite understandably so, considering that he was fighting for his reputation and his career – failing utterly to reflect, even for a moment, that all this solemn argument was about such trivia as a single swearword, an admiral's fit of pique, and a suitcase or two that nearly got a soaking, and Collard, whose behaviour was just as singular, alternating between moments of bristling antagonism and flares of ill-temper, mingled with careless nonchalance and high good humour, so much so that it was difficult at times to divine his temper. In truth, the Rear-Admiral was merely being himself, without any acknowledgement to Fate or to the court martial board that he was a very junior flag officer whose own career was just as much on trial, even if no formal charge was against his name.

The court had met with the idea of deciding on the rights and wrongs of composing or passing on a letter to a superior officer describing an admiral's conduct as vindictive. And its members were of little doubt, being honest men, brought up in the tradition of the Royal Navy, that, short of a remarkable defence, one that none of them could even visualize, retribution would be swift and punitive. Instead of which they had been treated to a rigmarole of petty bickering that would have been out of place in a midshipman's gunroom. But more painful, worse, far more painful, was the fact that all this nonsense, cheerful gossip for a wardroom though it might be, was being aired in public. Up in the temporary gallery rigged in *Eagle*'s hangar were a whole rank of reporters taking down every word.

It was possible to stand up in court and, by craning one's neck, to see all round the immaculate, pale grey, painted majesty of the proudest fleet in what was still the world's greatest navy. And now it was about to become a laughing stock, for every question by Dewar, every tart or sardonic answer by Collard, was being transmitted to London, to the popular press and to Parliament. Heaven only knew what those foreign journalists up in the gallery would write. The members of the court were not the only senior officers deeply concerned. Roger Keyes, the Commander-in-Chief himself, was a very hot tip for the ultimate naval appointment, that of First Sea Lord. Was it possible that this idiotic and widely publicized court martial could affect even his career? There were already those who wondered.

The court had tried its best to shut Dewar up when he first began to cross-examine Collard. He had answered by waving that confounded letter from the Admiralty at them. But now that the man's line of questioning meant dragging Collard's definition of discipline into the arena, it was worth another effort at shutting him up. So the President, Rear-Admiral Townsend, asked Dewar to stick to the charges – Collard's views on discipline had no bearing on them. Dewar tried to argue that they had, but Townsend said emphatically that such matters would be decided by the court. Dewar demanded that a protest objecting to the limitations placed on him should be entered in the minutes. Chief Petty Officer Writer William Barrett, whose onerous duty it had been to take a shorthand note of the day's proceedings, duly noted the objection.

Dewar turned once more to his Admiral. Now his concern was the conversation that took place when Collard personally delivered his and Daniel's letters to Vice-Admiral Kelly, Commander of the First Battle Squadron and the obvious president of any court of enquiry that might ensue.

Dewar: 'When you took my letter to the Vice-Admiral may I ask if you totally denied the truth of the incidents described therein?'

Collard: 'So far as I remember, the truth or otherwise of the incidents was not discussed between the Vice-Admiral and myself.'

Dewar: 'Did you make any counter-charges against me?'

'So far as I remember, I do not think that we discussed the subject matter in the letters at all.'

Dewar: 'Did you not say that I had been disloyal to you?'

Collard: 'At the enquiry I did.'

Dewar became both heated and adamant. 'I am not talking about the enquiry,' he insisted. 'Did you not say at this interview with the Vice-Admiral that I was disloyal to you?'

Collard was a complete match for his man. 'So far as I remember,' he retorted crisply, 'I did not. But I would not mind if I had.'

Now the Prosecutor got to his feet and pointed out that what passed between the Rear-Admiral and Vice-Admiral of the First Battle Squadron was a question of privilege and should not be dragged out in open court. The President agreed. He told Dewar that, in order to allow him full justice, they had let him go as far with his questioning as he had. Now it must stop. Dewar's reaction was to demand that it be noted that he protested because he was not allowed to pursue his particular line of cross-examination. Once more Chief Petty Officer Writer Barrett duly recorded the fact.

From this moment onwards the situation between Dewar and his Admiral degenerated even further. Collard insisted that if his Flag Captain had any complaint about the ship's discipline then he should have made a verbal report to him. In reply Dewar pointed out the instance of the Chaplain. When he made a verbal report, had he not been threatened with a court martial? Collard said the situation was entirely different. The Chaplain had no right to see him, whereas his Flag Captain had that right at any hour of the day or night. Anyway, he had not threatened the man with a court martial.

Dewar: 'Did you not, at the court of enquiry, accuse me of behaviour on the 9th of March, when the ship returned to Malta, which, if it had been true, would have been most disgraceful behaviour on my part?'

Collard: 'I did.'

Dewar: 'May I ask, then, why you did not tell this court the account of this incident when you were asked for specific examples of my disloyalty?'

Collard: 'When was I asked for specific examples of your disloyalty?'

The question was repeated. This time the Admiral answered, 'I gave the court of enquiry this incident to show how little help you were to me as a flag captain and chief staff officer, not as an instance of your disloyalty.'

Pressed harder by Dewar, Collard gave his version of the episode of the buoys. *Royal Oak*, he said, and *Ramillies* were detailed by the harbour authorities for their respective buoys when they entered harbour the next day. *Royal Oak* was to go to No. 12 buoy, *Ramillies* to No. 13, which was nearest the entrance to the harbour, No. 12 being abreast of the aircraft carrier *Eagle*, the very ship in which they were now giving evidence. As *Royal Oak* was taking the inner berth, Collard had left orders that she was to enter harbour first. But at some time during the night the orders were changed and the buoy numbers reversed. Collard said that either he had not been told of the alteration or that he had not noticed. Had he done so he would have ordered *Ramillies* into harbour first. The next day *Royal Oak* led the way and headed for No. 13, the buoy by the harbour mouth. Collard, who was on his bridge, turned to his Flag Lieutenant and asked why his flagship was going to the wrong buoy. The Flag Lieutenant asked the bridge below, where Dewar was stationed, and was told the order had been changed. Collard had great difficulty, he told the court, from stopping *Ramillies* entering harbour, for by now *Royal Oak* was lying across her course as she manoeuvred into position. Finally *Ramillies* had to pick her way to her buoy through an unnecessarily narrow space between *Eagle* and *Royal Oak*. Collard's contention was that he had cited this incident to the original court of enquiry just to show that, if he had had a flag captain who watched his interests, then Dewar would have gone to him and said that *Royal Oak* and *Ramillies* were entering harbour in the wrong order. Collard felt that he had been let down.

His answers to Dewar's cross-examination on this point can only be described as most extraordinary.

Dewar: 'I put it to you that the signal log was shown to you by the Flag Lieutenant at 8 a.m. on Friday morning?'

Collard: 'I dare say.'

Dewar: 'I put it to you that your signature is now in the log?'

Collard: 'I dare say.'

Dewar: 'I put it to you that you saw the signal?'

Collard: 'I could have if I had wished to.'

Dewar: 'I put it to you that you saw the signal?'

Collard: 'I do not know whether I saw it or not or even whether I saw the signal log that morning.'

Dewar: 'I put it to you that your signature is in the signal log just below this very signal?'

Collard: 'The fact that I initial the signal log does not mean that I read every signal or even one third of the signals. It merely shows that I have seen the signal log at a certain time.'

Dewar: 'Do you think that I was correct in assuming that this signal had been shown to you?'

Collard: 'Yes, I do.'

Now the prosecution objected. Dewar's line of cross-examination dealt with an incident that had occurred after the writing of the letters which were the subject of the charges and therefore was in no way relevant. But there was no stopping Dewar. He persisted in asking Collard if it was a fact that the Admiral normally dealt with the navigating commander where a question of berthing was concerned. Collard agreed it was.

Dewar: 'Is it not a fact that, after securing, you did not mention this incident to me but sent for the navigating commander?'

Collard: 'I talked to the navigating commander about it on the bridge.'

Dewar: 'Did you mention it to me at any time?'

Collard: 'I was proposing to mention it to you that afternoon, but, after you left those letters with me, I decided that any more fault-finding with you that afternoon would be injudicious and it could wait.'

Dewar came to the last of his long list of questions. He asked Collard if, under the circumstances just described, the Admiral thought it had been fair of him to tell the court of enquiry that the Captain's behaviour on that occasion was an example of deliberate disloyalty.

Collard replied emphatically, 'I do'.

Dewar thanked him politely and the duel between Admiral and Captain was finally over.

Now it was the prosecution's turn to re-examine. Only a few questions were asked, but they most certainly underlined the court's attitude to an admiral's standing in the order of things and its view on those who wrote complaining letters.

Rear-Admiral Dudley Boyle, the Prosecutor, adjusted his eyeglass, glanced at his notes and inquired of his brother Rear-Admiral: 'Who do you consider to be the person most interested in the world to see that your best uniform comes safely up the ladder?'

Collard: 'I consider that I was.'

Prosecutor: 'In your judgment is an admiral able to decide whether he shall have his barge hoisted in or not?'

Collard: 'Entirely able to judge.'

Prosecutor: 'Do you consider an admiral has the right to take charge anywhere if he sees fit?'

Collard: 'Yes I do. Anywhere.'

Prosecutor: 'A question was asked that you were somewhat bothered about "Who had given an order for the barge to come to the port side?" Do you consider it the practice of the Service for the admiral to order the barge which side he likes?'

Collard: 'Entirely.'

13

'A Malevolent Conspiracy'

FREDERICK ANTREE WESTON was then summoned before the court. Straight-backed, stiff-necked and as superbly turned out as befitted the master-at-arms of one of His Majesty's flagships and the disciplinary lord and master of the lower deck of *Royal Oak*, he gave it as his opinion that the general conduct of the ship's company was average by Royal Naval standards, though he agreed in cross-examination that he had heard rumours on the mess deck that the Admiral had told the Captain that he was no more use to him than a bloody midshipman. That, he felt, had done nothing for the Captain's standing among the crew. And that, too, closed the case for the prosecution.

Captain Dewar asked Kimball to make the opening speech for the defence and, bewigged and gowned, the American-born lawyer, who had had little or nothing to do all that day, made the most of his opportunity. As usual he addressed the court at considerable length. The court in return, starch-collared, frock-coated, gilded and burdened with shoulder bullion, fiddled with its white gloves and swords and made every effort to concentrate.

Put simply, Kimball's case was that Dewar was being tried because he had forwarded Commander Daniel's letter. There was no suggestion that his own covering letter was at fault. But, as it contained many of the points that Daniel had made, then surely Daniel's letter was also justified? The Commander had been asked to write the letter in the first place. True, he had added several paragraphs of his own volition, but they were intended for the good of the welfare and discipline of the ship. Dewar had accepted the letter after being certain in his own mind that Daniel had given its composition serious thought and had no alternative but to forward it. He was in no way intended to be a censor.

Dewar then gave evidence himself. He said that he had no personal feeling in writing his own letter of complaint about Collard. In fact, he realized that making a personal report like that on a superior was not likely to do him any good. He did not make a personal protest to Collard himself because 'I considered then and I consider now that, if I went with a protest of that sort to Admiral Collard in his cabin, that he would at once have lost his temper and probably threatened me with a court martial for bringing complaints against a flag officer'.

Dewar spoke very highly of Daniel. He repeated the evidence he had given at the Commander's court martial, namely that when he had joined *Royal Oak* he had found the ship outwardly efficient but dead – no enthusiasm and no life. In one month Daniel had entirely changed the ship's spirit. He had implicit confidence in Daniel's ability and considered him the best executive officer he had ever met. And never had he met an officer whose morals and honour he would trust more.

Now it was the prosecution's turn to cross-examine Dewar as thoroughly as he had questioned his own Admiral earlier on. It did not take long to get down to the heart of things.

Prosecutor: 'Now, as regards the coming-on-board incident, what exactly do you complain of in the Admiral's conduct – not saluting you or returning your salute?'

Dewar: 'I consider that for an officer to come on board in front of a large number of officers and men, with the Captain and other officers standing at the salute and for that officer to approach without returning the salute, without paying any attention to them whatever is, to say the least of it, humiliating.'

Prosecutor: 'Will you agree with me that of two men, one of whom behaves correctly and the other incorrectly, then the humiliation is not to the one who behaves correctly?'

Dewar: 'I don't agree with you under the circumstances.'

Prosecutor: 'Then we are to understand that the fact that your salute was not returned created this incident and humiliated you?'

Dewar: 'I don't agree. I considered it an insult.'

Prosecutor: 'Was it not a very trivial incident?'

Dewar: 'That is a matter of opinion and I did not think it trivial.'

Changing the subject, Dewar was asked that, if a captain of a ship had a very serious report made to him by his executive officer, was he to accept that report without verifying it. The accused answered that he should not. Well then, what steps had he taken to verify Daniel's report that the Admiral's conduct had a serious effect on discipline and morale in *Royal Oak*?

Dewar's answer did not help his case at all. 'I did not meticulously examine every word of his letter,' he said. 'To my mind it helped me to explain to the Vice-Admiral the result of these incidents. I thought it was obvious it would have a bad effect and I asked the Commander if that was really his opinion. I felt I had to rely on the Commander in this sort of matter.' Then he added that he was quite ready to admit that a part of Daniel's letter might have been too expressive.

Prosecutor: 'So you forwarded this letter to the Vice-Admiral making these insinuations against you and your own ship's company without examining every word?'

Dewar: 'I did not consider it my duty to alter the wording of a letter. I asked the Commander if he was sure he wanted this letter forwarded. I do not think it is the duty of a captain to tinker with the phraseology of a letter submitted to him for passing on to a senior officer.'

Prosecutor: 'Is it really your view that you cannot censor a letter sent you by a junior?'

Dewar: 'In a case like this, I consider the captain has either to forward the letter or not forward it. The words of the regulation are that he is to forward, in his discretion, such letters as he thinks best for the good of the Service.'

Prosecutor: 'Where do you stop? Would you let any expression be used and sent forward?'

Dewar: 'No. Certainly not.'

Prosecutor: 'How far would you allow an officer to go?'

Dewar: 'When I consider it my duty to explain, secretly and in confidence, to a senior officer the effect of certain incidents in a ship, and so long as the letter is limited to describing the effect of these incidents and does not contain unnecessary criticisms of a senior, I see no objection in forwarding it, providing the writer honestly believes what he has written.'

Prosecutor: 'How can you know, without going into the letter word by word, what is in the letter?'

Dewar: 'I did read the letter through and I thought that it conveyed fairly accurate particulars which would help the Vice-Admiral to appreciate the situation.'

Prosecutor: 'You have given a glowing account of Commander Daniel's service to you in *Royal Oak*?'

Dewar: 'Yes.'

Prosecutor: 'Did you not warn him of the risk he was running in putting such expressions into a letter?'

Dewar: 'I did not think for one moment that a letter of complaint sent forward in good faith would be turned round into a charge against the complainant. I looked on that letter as a secret letter and I was quite unable to tell the course of events which have followed it.'

Dewar was then asked what action, after all his years of service, he thought would ensue from sending on the letters. He answered that he had imagined that either one of two things would occur. He thought it likely that Collard would read the letters, then send for him and talk it over. Collard would admit that such situations as the letters described were intolerable and that the letters themselves would go no further. An even more likely outcome would be that Vice-Admiral Kelly would send for both himself and Collard. Then Collard would be asked if the incidents were true and that Collard would admit that, in substance, they were.

By the time Dewar gave this last answer the harsh, glaring overhead lights had been burning bright for some time, making the hollow, echoing hangar look an even bleaker place than it was by day.

It had been yet another long day. At seven o'clock that evening the court was adjourned. Chief Petty Officer Writer Barrett must have laid down his shorthand pencil with a considerable sense of relief.

It was a relief to know that tomorrow should see an end to these courts martial. At last the impatiently waiting fleet would be able to sail on its spring cruise and enjoy the much-delayed junketing, the balls, the shipboard dances, the fireworks and the festivities of all its ports of call in Spain and the south of France. But, in view of the most unseasonably nasty weather, the delay might have been opportune. The sky next day, Thursday, was no more promising.

When the court re-assembled at 9.30 in the morning, *Eagle*'s immaculately-spread deck awnings were snapping and cracking in half a gale and sheets of rain came slanting down.

The proceedings started in singular and unorthodox fashion. Quite out of turn, Dewar stood up and made a speech. 'Before this case re-opens,' he said, 'I would like to submit to the court that the defence wish to cut this case as short as possible and they intend to cut down the witnesses to the very minimum. And they intend to limit the questions to the minimum necessary to prove the facts set out in the letter and hope that this will not be regarded as any admission of weakness in the evidence, because it is based on the belief that there can be no serious doubt as to the facts set out in that letter. In making this proposal the defence hope that the prosecution will reciprocate and will, as far as possible, limit their questions to prove the actual charges set forth in the charge sheet.'

Rear-Admiral William Boyle, the Prosecutor, did not rise to this bait. He wisely said nothing in reply and waited to resume his cross-examination of the Captain.

Boyle's first question was to refer Dewar to his answer the night before. 'In view of your previous experience with Admiral Collard, did you hope he would do anything rather than take that letter to the Vice-Admiral?' Dewar replied, 'I thought it quite possible he would discuss it with me first. In fact I was almost certain he would.'

Prosecutor: 'You make a definite statement: "A great deal of discontent on the lower deck," and I ask you if you will agree that it is exaggerated?'

Dewar: 'No, I will not. But I don't for one minute pretend that it had produced anything in the manner that would lead to any manifestation, any definite action. I don't pretend that for one minute.'

Prosecutor: 'Will you agree that is a somewhat unusual and alarming state of affairs in a British battleship?'

Dewar: 'It is not intended to be alarming at all. I intended to convey, secretly, my opinion to the Vice-Admiral of the effect of these incidents on the ship.'

Prosecutor: 'Would you agree with me that, if this was reported as the state of affairs existing, it would call for immediate action by higher authority?'

Dewar: 'That is a matter of opinion. Personally, if it had been a case of that sort referred to me, my immediate action would have been to send for the officers concerned and inquire of them.'

The prosecution then warmed to its task of giving the accused a rough time of it. Despite his protests that it had nothing to do with the charge, he was forced to confess he had taken no action to alleviate the lower deck discontent that he alleged existed.

Prosecutor: 'In Paragraph 11 of your letter you state that in future the ship would be your first consideration. What had been your first consideration up to that time?'

Dewar: 'What I meant by that was that, if, on any future occasion, similar incidents occurred, my desire to avoid any scandal affecting the Flag Officer would be overridden by the necessity of considering the interests of the ship and of the Service as a whole, irrespective of any individual.'

The prosecution made strenuous efforts to establish that Dewar had colluded in the contents of his Commander's letter. How much discussion had taken place between them before it was written? Why had the Commander shown his Captain a draft of the letter before it was written? Was Dewar in the habit of receiving letters from subordinate officers in draft form? The accused could only answer that it had been a novel experience for him. He had never asked for a letter before.

Prosecutor: 'Now what is the object of showing anyone letters in draft form?'

Dewar: 'Presumably to see whether they approve of it.'

Prosecutor: 'So that they can review it?'

Dewar: 'Perhaps it would save time if I just tell you . . .'

Prosecutor: 'I don't think it would, really.'

Dewar: 'Commander Daniel's letter consisted of two parts. The second part contained remarks on a subject which I suggested he should make to me, and he brought those remarks to me . . . and showed them to me. I looked through them and said words to the effect, "Now, are you sure you want these remarks to go in?" and he said, "Yes". There is no mystery about this letter. In accepting Commander Daniel's letter – and will you please note that the word "Accept" is used in both charges against me – I am supposed to have approved generally of what was in it.'

Prosecutor: 'Did you or did you not consider that it represented the general state of affairs existing on board?'

Dewar: 'I considered it represented, in somewhat expressive form, the state of affairs which I thought extremely probable, but if I had thought it was going to anyone else but the Rear-Admiral and the Vice-Admiral, in a privileged form, it would have been altered.'

Prosecutor: 'Might I ask if "expressive form" means exaggerated form?'

Dewar: 'Not necessarily. It means some people express things in different ways.'

Now Admiral Boyle pressed home the point he had always been determined to make, that Daniel's letter was a conspiracy between the flagship's Captain and Commander against their Rear-Admiral.

'Will you allow,' he asked, 'that, in reality, Commander Daniel's letter was your letter?'

Dewar was adamant. 'I will allow nothing of the sort. Why should I? It was a separate letter signed by him.'

Why had Dewar's secretary had to retype his own letter twice? What alterations had been made? Dewar said he could not remember. 'But,' he added, 'I can tell you that if I write an important letter on some particular subject I may write as many as twenty drafts and the fact that this letter was only typed twice is not extraordinary.'

Prosecutor: 'Let me quote the last few lines of Commander Daniel's letter: "My recent appeal to look forward to the coming inspection, thereby making it serve a useful purpose for the efficiency of the Service, has been reversed by the anticipation of vindictive fault-finding." Do you consider that was a proper thing to add in a letter of reasons in writing for the Admiral to see?'

Dewar: 'I tried to explain this letter consisted of two parts. In Paragraph 9 Commander Daniel says, "This ends my report". The second part of this letter is not reasons in writing. I have said that at least half-a-dozen times.'

Dewar then set about the extremely difficult task of trying to convince the court that Daniel's letter had not accused Collard of being vindictive or even that Daniel thought that he would be when the forthcoming inspection took place, merely that the ship's company thought that he would be. He certainly did not convince Rear-Admiral Boyle for the prosecution. Dewar went so far as to say that if Daniel had accused Collard of any intention of fault-finding, then he would have corrected him. By saying that he once more opened the door to attack.

Boyle: 'Did you feel you were bound to forward this letter to the Rear-Admiral?'

Dewar: 'I did. It was a matter within my discretion as laid down in Article 9.'

Boyle: 'If it was in your discretion, you were not bound to do it?'

Dewar: 'My discretion decided I was bound to do it.'

Boyle: 'Would not it have been more kind and considerate to have made your complaint without dragging Daniel into it?'

Now Dewar made his great confession. In answer to that question he said, 'I asked Commander Daniel if he was sure he wanted his letter forwarded and he said he did, but if I had thought for one moment this letter was going to be turned round into a charge, I assure you Commander Daniel's letter would not have gone in.'

By such a reply Dewar underlined in the most startling fashion how he had misread Collard's hot-tempered nature, right from the moment he had become his Flag Captain. Whatever Collard was, he was most certainly not the man to knuckle down to threats. Any young midshipman with the least understanding of human nature would have placed a large bet, or as large as gunroom pay would permit, on that!

Automatically Collard would have done exactly what he did do when the letters were thumped on his desk by Dewar. After a few hours of reflection he flew into a rage of self-justification and headed for higher authority.

Boyle was not going to let Dewar off the hook after his last admission. He asked, 'Then in the light of subsequent evidence it is your opinion that it was ill-advised to have forwarded Commander Daniel's letter?'

Dewar: 'I don't say ill-advised. I am certainly extremely sorry I did.'

Boyle was now on the rampage. He made Dewar admit he had not consulted any other flag officer in the Mediterranean Fleet about the situation aboard *Royal Oak*, nor had he sought the advice of fellow captains, even though he was in the habit of going for long walks ashore with them. In fairness to himself, Dewar made it clear that he felt it would be improper to discuss Collard behind his back, and that on one occasion he had thought of approaching Vice-Admiral Kelly but rejected the idea for the same reason.

Boyle: 'Is it a fair statement of the salient points in your letter and that of Commander Daniel as they would appear to an administrative authority:

1. The Admiral and the Captain were at loggerheads.
2. The Commander was in support of the Captain.
3. The officers were deeply indignant and resentful.
4. There was great discontent on the lower deck.
5. That a very serious effect had been produced on discipline and morale.
6. The ship was discouraged?

'Before you answer, I would point out the last four are all definite statements.'

Dewar's reply was tart: 'In view of the fact that the administrative authority apparently read that I had entered into some sort of a plot or conspiracy to get rid of Admiral Collard, I am not prepared to say what view they would have taken of my letter.'

Boyle: 'Do you consider it would have been possible for the Commander-in-Chief, after receiving your letter and that of Commander Daniel, to leave Commander Daniel, yourself and Admiral Collard in the same ship?'

The court intervened to save Daniel from answering what was, after all, a hypothetical question concerning the Commander-in-Chief.

Boyle tried again. 'What I wished to ask the accused,' he said, rephrasing his question, 'was if he considered it in the best interests of the Service to leave Commander Daniel, himself and Admiral Collard in the same ship, after the incidents had occurred?'

Dewar: 'Well my reply to that is that question is a most misleading one. I didn't say that at the present moment there was a good deal of discontent on the lower deck, nor did I say there was intense indignation or disgust among officers. What I said was the attack on the Bandmaster two months before had that effect. I didn't say when I sent in my letter, nor did I intend to convey the impression that the ship was in a state of latent mutiny, and that, if something was not done, something would happen. You have twisted my words to mean something different from what I said.'

Both Prosecutor and accused were tiring by now and the cross-examination ended on a fractious note.

Boyle: 'Do you not agree with me that the bearing of the officer commanding has a great deal to do with the discipline of the ship?'

Dewar: 'What do you mean by bearing exactly?'

Boyle: 'I will explain. I would like to use words of poetry: "Laugh and the world laughs with you". Would that explain it?'

Dewar: 'No, I am afraid it doesn't. Do you mean if I had gone about laughing it would have made a difference?'

Boyle: 'I think it would have made a lot of difference. I mean if the situation had been faced and you had shown there was no need for any discontent on your behalf, there would have been no indiscipline in the ship of any sort.'

Dewar promptly appealed to the court for support. 'May I ask the court,' he exclaimed, 'whether it is relevant, in this case, to discuss what I should have done and whether, had my bearing been different, the discipline of the ship would not have been affected?'

The court gave it as its opinion that the questions were relevant. But, it added stiffly, those questions should be in a shorter form and less involved. Admiral Boyle, clearly nettled, asked if that ruling would also apply to the answers. He was told that it would.

With that, Boyle suddenly declared that the prosecution had no more questions to ask.

Kimball then rose to re-examine.

'Are there any charges against you about your own letter?' was one of the questions he asked Dewar. The accused replied, 'No. I wrote an official letter to the Admiralty, begging them that I might be tried for writing and forwarding an unjustifiable letter of complaint. The reply of the Admiralty was that they did not see their way to add that to my charges. I wished to clear my character from the imputation of forwarding or writing an unjustifiable complaint.'

Daniel took Dewar's place as witness. Today he was wearing his sword again. His punishment was still to be ratified by the Admiralty. When that happened, as it most surely would, he would be stranded ashore on half-pay until, and if ever, it was decided to offer him a fresh appointment. But, until that ratification of his sentence, he was still attached to the depot ship HMS *Cormorant*.

Boyle, in cross-examination, wanted to know why Daniel had not done more to check the wardroom gossip over Collard's behaviour at the dance and the ensuing incidents. He quoted one of the Navy's idols, Admiral of the Fleet Sir John Jervis, Earl of St Vincent, on what he had to say about mutiny: 'I dread not the seamen. It is the indiscreet, licentious conversation of officers that produces all our ills.' Daniel rallied well. 'I don't recognize the quotation,' he retorted, 'but it is extremely appropriate, for licentious remarks of the officer in question were responsible for the state of affairs which prevailed.'

Referring to that state of affairs, he cited the example of one senior officer indignantly describing Collard's language at the dance by saying, 'He might just as well have called my wife a tart.'

Daniel added, 'There was a feeling in the wardroom the like of which I have never experienced. For that reason I felt that highly coloured language was necessary to convey an accurate picture to the Captain.'

The Reverend Harry Goulding, *Royal Oak*'s Chaplain, was also called to give evidence on Dewar's behalf. He said he had asked to see Collard because earlier in the day he had been in his own cabin discussing the music for the forthcoming Sunday church service with the Bandmaster when Barnacle had broken down. He was in great distress over the language that the Admiral had used to him.

'I wished to explain to the Admiral,' Goulding told the court, 'what I was sure he had not understood, namely that he had insulted, very cruelly, someone not in a position to reply.'

Goulding went on, 'Rear-Admiral Collard told me there were very serious penalties inflicted on those who made accusations against flag officers. He said, "I'll have you court-martialled." I said, "Do you really wish to send for the Captain, because I came to ask your advice and also to prevent mischief, not to make further mischief?" I explained that, in the minds of a number of people, he had insulted someone in the presence of ladies very cruelly, who was not in a position to reply.'

In answer to Kimball, who asked if Collard had sent for the Captain, the Chaplain replied, 'He made a dive for the bell on his desk, but missed it.'

Goulding, who must have been either a very brave man or exceedingly rash in his bearding of the infuriated Admiral, said that, after the incident of the bell, 'I asked him if he really wished to send for the Captain as I was dealing with facts well authenticated.'

Kimball: 'What was his condition?'

Goulding: 'In the greater part of the interview he was out of control. I had the greatest difficulty myself in remaining in the cabin.'

Goulding stated that a number of men of various ranks had been to see him and had expressed high indignation with what they thought had been an abuse of power. 'I don't think,' he said, 'that anyone expressed a complaint about the actual term used. That was more or less a technical matter.'

As for the wardroom officers, the Chaplain said they were furious. 'I heard,' he told the court, 'the Admiral alluded to in very offensive ways, so I was obliged to stop it. I heard him called a bloody little swine.'

Boyle now had his turn for the prosecution. He decided to deal with the matter of the word 'bugger'.

'What do you mean,' he asked Goulding, 'about the term used being a technical matter?'

Goulding: 'Well, it is very common in conversation.'

Boyle: 'Yes. It is used rather more frequently at sea than among the community of men and women on shore.'

Goulding: 'Well, it is used almost exclusively, I believe, among men.'

Boyle: 'Would it surprise you very much to know that some of *Royal Oak*'s petty officers first learnt that there was trouble in their ship from the London papers?'

Goulding: 'I know that is so.'

Now the court took a hand. The President asked: 'Are the men in *Royal Oak* discontented now?'

Goulding: 'They are feeling this very deeply. There are very evident signs, but they are behaving very sensibly about it. They are a very sensible ship's company.'

It was time for luncheon. The board members retired to the mahogany table in the Flag Officer's day cabin. The accused, his lawyer, witnesses, Press and spectators, stepped out on a rain-soaked deck to face the Levant, the local wind, now blowing at full force and blustering the clouds down from The Rock itself.

When everyone had returned to the temporary court room – some having fared better than others – Commander Brownlow, *Royal Oak*'s navigating commander and senior officer under Dewar, was called. He said that his Captain had told him more than once to try to anticipate Collard's wishes and intentions. He still believed that Daniel's letter was a fair statement of the feeling of the mess at the time.

Boyle: 'Was the feeling really so high?'

Brownlow: 'Mine was so high that I couldn't even discuss the matter.'

There were other witnesses, including the redoubtable Major Attwood, Royal Marines, who made it quite clear that he bitterly resented Collard's slur on his Corps. Then the defence's case was almost at an end. All that was left was the final address and Dewar was determined to make that himself. He was not going to leave his career in the hands of Kimball.

But it was Kimball who asked for a two hours' recess so that Dewar could prepare himself. This was granted and on a soggy, dismal Maundy Thursday the court once more retired to kick its heels.

But its members were better off than the spectators, including Mrs Dewar and Mrs Daniel. They had nothing but the chill walls of the aircraft hangar to look at.

No one expected a brief final speech from Captain Dewar, nor did they get one. As he had explained earlier, he was a man given to drafting any statement that he made, with patience and considerable care. It would not have been in the least surprising if he had been planning his final address to the court even before leaving England. Yet, for all its length, it was far from long-drawn-out or boring. One well-known counsel, after reading a verbatim report of the speech, doubted if any civilian lawyer could have argued even half so well. Dewar, in his quietly modulated voice and retiring manner, attacked from his very first word, or almost his first word.

He opened by defining the charges against him. 'In each of the two charges,' he said, 'I am accused of an act to the prejudice of good order and naval discipline, in that I accepted and forwarded a letter from Commander Daniel. In the first charge it is stated that the terms of the letter were subversive of discipline and in the second charge that the letter was contrary to Article 11 of King's Regulations, in that it contained remarks and criticisms of the conduct or orders of my superior officer.

'I would first like to draw the attention of the court to the fact that words – the following words – are omitted from the charge, although they are an extract from Article 11, and in fact form an essential part of it: "Which may bring him into contempt".'

Dewar submitted that this was a most important point, that the vital, qualifying sentence should have been so omitted from the charge. He pointed out that when Kimball, in his opening address, had declared that no one had been brought into contempt, the Deputy Judge Advocate had made an extraordinary admission. He said, in effect, that it was not necessary to prove contempt because the words were not included in the charge.

'Now, Sir,' demanded Dewar of the President, 'what would you think if the police wished to convict a man with being on enclosed premises with intent to commit a felony, and, finding that they had not sufficient evidence of his intention, they framed an indictment charging him only with being on enclosed premises? I submit that these two cases are identical. What do you think the Judge would do? What do you think the Court of Appeal would do? Learned counsel tells me that the omission from the charge of this vital, qualifying sentence is quite sufficient to invalidate the whole charge. If I may, I will read you a few lines from *Lectures on Naval Law and Court-Martial Procedure*. On page 15: "There is an essential principle in every charge, before any court that can exist in the civilized world, that the charge should be sufficiently specific to enable the accused to know what he is to answer, and to enable the court to know what they are called to inquire into." I am charged under Article 11, on a matter of forwarding a letter containing remarks and criticisms. But Article 11 does not say that. It says that no one shall make or pass criticisms or remarks on their superiors which tend to bring them into contempt. I submit to the court that the omission of this sentence is a most serious defect in the charge.'

Dewar told the court that the prosecution, in its eagerness to obtain a conviction, had overlooked an elementary principle of justice. Furthermore, in an effort to make a mountain out of a molehill, it had magnified one charge into two. After all, if Daniel's letter was subversive of discipline, it could only be so by being in contravention of Article 11. That was to say because it contained criticisms or remarks on the conduct of his superior officer.

'If that is so,' argued Dewar, 'then the first charge is contained in the second, and if the second charge fails, the first charge must also fail. It is an excellent thing for the prosecution to have two strings to its bow, but in this case it has provided only one arrow.'

Dewar went on to say that the question as to whether the forwarding of Daniel's letter was prejudicial to good order and naval discipline must depend on the circumstances that led up to the remarks in that letter and the motives that inspired Dewar to forward it. He had described those circumstances in his own covering letter.

'Is that letter true or is it not?' he demanded. 'Was there, as Rear-Admiral Collard would have you believe, a malevolent conspiracy on the part of Commander Daniel and myself to drive him out of the ship?'

Dewar pointed out that a great deal of evidence had been given as to the facts in his own letter. He did not propose to go into them for it would be wasting the court's time as they were obviously true. And that the court must know.

'Opposed to this mass of evidence,' he said, 'we merely have the statement of Rear-Admiral Collard. And it is highly significant that the prosecution has not produced one single witness in support of the Rear-Admiral's account. The idea of a captain of my seniority trumping up a series of charges against his admiral is, I submit, simply absurd. What could I hope to gain by such conduct?'

14

Personal Honour

THE ACCUSED CAPTAIN WAS IN FULL FLOW now and treating the court martial board to a most unusual display of forensic skill. He justified his forwarding of the two letters by claiming that Collard's behaviour was prejudicial to *Royal Oak*'s discipline. It caused criticism of the Admiral himself. Criticism of a superior officer was forbidden by Article 11 of King's Regulations. The only way to stop that criticism, in Dewar's opinion, was to stop such incidents happening again. He told the court that it was paradoxical that he should now be tried for forwarding a letter criticizing a superior officer when one of his main objects was to stop a recurrence of such criticism. Furthermore, even if the letters contained criticism of Collard, they went only to the Vice-Admiral and Collard himself, whereas the main comment on Collard's conduct was being broadcast throughout the ship and was much more subversive of discipline.

'We have heard,' said Dewar, his voice strong, 'the prosecution heckling witnesses as to whether they noticed any signs of disaffection in the ship; whether the men drilled properly, whether they were clean and so on. Only last night I was told that my letter was viewed as a "frame up" in certain quarters, because, in actual fact, the discipline of the *Royal Oak*'s men was proved to be quite good. Apparently some people have interpreted my letter to mean that the incidents had introduced into the ship a state of latent mutiny. The thought never entered my mind.'

Dewar explained that quite obviously his idea of discipline was not the same as that of the Prosecutor. Dewar believed in a reciprocal relationship between all ranks which brought about the most willing, efficient and intelligent co-operation. Nothing was more destructive of that than the bullying and abuse of subordinates.

'I have no doubt,' he said pointedly, 'that the court is acquainted with Article 7 of King's Regulations, which definitely forbids bullying or undeserved abuse or irritating language, especially towards inferiors.'

It was at this point, unfortunately, that Dewar seemed to get carried away with his argument. Goodness knows who he had been listening to back in his hotel after the court had adjourned the previous evening, but what had been said had, without any question, stirred him considerably.

'There is another point I should like to mention,' he went on, 'which I heard from a high source last night. I heard for the first time that some clever people have connected my letter complaining of the effect of Admiral Collard's behaviour on discipline with the scare headlines that appeared in the Press immediately after I got back here. [He meant on his return to the Mediterranean Fleet after he had been sent home to England]: "Mutiny in the *Royal Oak*". Apparently they credit me with having put it in the paper. It hardly seems worth while denying such rubbish.'

Dewar then tried hard to reason with the court. 'I treated the Rear-Admiral as a highly honoured guest in the ship. How could I hope to maintain my authority if he attacked me in this manner? Being convinced that these incidents had to be stopped, I ask the court to consider what they would have done under the circumstances. I might have made a verbal protest of course. I considered that. My judgement and my previous experience told me that that would be ineffective.

'You have heard the evidence of the Chaplain, and I think that confirms the soundness of my judgement. You heard him say he found it a hard time, even staying in the cabin. I knew that if I went personally to the Rear-Admiral on this matter, I would merely have been bullied. Again, I might have gone privately to the Vice-Admiral or some other officer, but I don't believe in creeping up the back stairs. I don't think it is right that any officer should go behind the back of his senior officer and carry reports of his conduct. I never mentioned any of these incidents to any officer in the Fleet simply because I thought it would be an improper thing to do.'

Dewar said that he considered that the only course open to him was to follow King's Regulations and write a formal letter to Vice-Admiral Kelly. To that effect he consulted Daniel.

'If a captain is not entitled to consult and utilize the opinion of his commander in such a matter,' he protested, 'how can he be held responsible for the discipline and morale of his ship?'

Dewar made a confession to the court. He admitted, he said, that while he had very carefully drafted and re-drafted his own letter, he had not meticulously examined every word of Daniel's to see if anything was liable to misinterpretation.

'I didn't think then and I do not think now,' he added, 'that the form of the Commander's letter was a matter of very vital importance.'

Dewar submitted, however, that the evidence which had been produced showed that Daniel's letter did paint a true picture of the situation.

'You have heard,' he argued, 'the evidence of at least four officers on that point. The prosecution have not attempted to produce a single witness to contradict the facts stated in that letter. Do you mean to tell me that they have not tried to find officers who would say the facts and statements in these letters were untrue? Of course they have!

'Why have they not found officers who would tell you that the wardroom was not inflamed with indignation? Isn't that sufficient proof that it was?'

Perhaps it was the stony faces of the judging officers lining the table before him or the seeming indifference to what he regarded as simple logic, but Dewar allowed some bitterness to show through his words.

'In view of the fact that I was ignominiously turned out of the *Royal Oak*, it is to be expected that I was guilty of some crime – of conspiracy, disloyalty, malice, vindictiveness, or even of uncharitableness – but not one scrap of evidence has been produced by the prosecution to show that Commander Daniel and I were not loyal to the Admiral, in thought, word and deed . . . In making this complaint and forwarding Commander Daniel's letter, I was actuated solely by a sense of duty. It was certainly not to my advantage to bring a complaint against my Rear-Admiral. I bore no malice against him. I bear none now. I am extremely sorry for him and I feel nothing he has done deserved this candle which this case holds to his name. At the same time, I would recall, he brought a good deal of challenges against me.'

Once again Dewar referred to conversations he had had after the previous day's hearing. Whatever his brother officer 'friends' had told him quite clearly rankled.

'Only last night,' he protested, 'I heard from some senior officer that I am supposed to have worked with Commander Daniel to hunt Admiral

Collard out of the ship. I have been told other things, which, if true, would be a disgrace to the uniform I wear. I know other serious charges have been brought against me about which I know nothing. I now, for the first time, understand why I was sent home in disgrace. I can only vaguely guess the object of such rumours, but I would ask the court to think that, in actual fact, I am not very different from themselves, and unless real evidence is produced to the contrary, I ask them to credit me with the same sense of honesty and decency as themselves.'

Dewar went on to argue the technical weaknesses of the case against him. He made many points. One of them concerned the first charge against him which referred to Daniel's letter as being subversive of discipline. Dewar wanted to know exactly whose discipline was being subverted. Was it his personally, for it was to him that Daniel handed the letter? Or was it that of Vice-Admiral Kelly who was to receive it?

And as far as he was accused of passing on that letter, it was, he put to the court, an analogous case. 'Supposing,' he said, 'a lieutenant of one of your ships wrote a letter to the commander complaining that you, the captain, had misconducted yourself in some way, and stating that your behaviour had inflamed the officers and men with indignation; he gives it to the commander and tells him definitely that he wants it forwarding to you. And supposing the commander did forward it. I put it to you, not one captain here would think of court-martialling, or even censuring, the commander for merely forwarding that letter. In so far as the charge is concerned, that is what I am accused of.'

Dewar ended his long address with a most impassioned plea. 'I was ignominiously turned out of my ship and sent home without knowing what I had done wrong. After thirty years my character and reputation had been ruined without any charge against me. I pressed for a court martial and, presumably because there was no evidence, I am now before you on the trivial charge of not having sufficiently censored a letter. I submit that there is no case against me. A great principle of justice is involved. I ask the court not only to acquit me, but to acquit me honourably as this case is one which affects my personal honour.'

It was six o'clock in the evening before Dewar sat down again.

It might have been a very fine speech, one that would have carried much weight before an ordinary judge and jury, and, as a dissertation on the principles of discipline, would been greeted as thought-provoking at a Staff College lecture, but it cut little ice with his fellow officers sitting in judgement. They had it firmly fixed in their minds that there would have been no need for all this court-martial nonsense, speechifying and publicity, if Dewar had only had the common sense to tell Commander Daniel to rephrase his letter and to have had a quiet and confidential word with some senior officer. Anyway, it was too late now. And it was time for the court to adjourn once more so that Rear-Admiral Boyle could prepare his reply for the prosecution. This took some while, and when Boyle finally rose he had hardly spoken a few words before, on the rainswept deck, the bugles rang out for the ritual of 'Sunset'. The whole court, accused and spectators, rose and stood facing the quarterdeck and waited in silence as a limp white ensign was hauled slowly down.

The interruption over, Boyle's speech turned out to be brief. He pointed out that it was Dewar himself who had asked to be court-martialled. He then went on to complain that the prosecution had been placed at a definite disadvantage because, throughout most of the case, the defence had been allowed to introduce matters that had nothing to do with the charges. Boyle argued that Collard's behaviour was irrelevant to either of the two charges brought against Dewar. What is more he was not going to refer to it. The mass of evidence on details should not be allowed to fog the issue, and the plea of justification on which the defence largely rested was itself a tacit admission that the offences had been committed.

Every unfounded rumour regarding the incidents had been exploited and many unfair and untrue innuendoes had been made. The Rear-Admiral had found fault, as he had a perfect right to do, when he discovered that his orders had not been carried out. The method of his fault-finding might, or might not, be open to question. Boyle closed his address by saying that the notoriety of the trial might well have been avoided by more deliberate reflection by the accused at the time of the incidents.

The moment for judgement had come. Dewar had called for the court martial and now he would see if his gamble with his career had succeeded.

Spectators, Press, witnesses, Dewar himself and the advocates were once more turned out of the hangar to find what shelter they could from the driving rain. They were kept waiting less than half an hour. When they returned their eyes turned automatically to the accused's sword lying on the table. The point was toward him.

Only Dewar appeared not to notice. He took his place, stiff and tight-lipped. Among the spectators, Mrs Dewar cried a little but very quietly.

It turned out to be a most unsatisfactory verdict. Dewar had been found guilty of the first charge of forwarding a letter whose contents were subversive of discipline, but he was acquitted on the second of forwarding a letter containing criticism of Collard's conduct and his orders.

Dewar declined to say anything in mitigation but merely handed in his certificates. These were even more impressive than Daniel's. They dated back to 1896. Two captains wrote of his bright promise as a midshipman. 'Zealous' was the word most often used to describe him as a lieutenant. He was a gunnery officer of the highest attainment and deserved quick promotion. One captain described him as 'An officer of excellent judgement who will do well in the higher ranks of the Service'. As Dewar rose to commander and then to captain, so the praise continued. But those certificates did nothing to sway the court's sentence. Dewar was dismissed his ship and severely reprimanded.

It must have been a morose group of the Dewars, Daniels and their lawyer who dined that miserable Maundy Thursday in Gibraltar's second best hotel. Sad save, perhaps, for Dewar himself. He was far too angry at the way Boyle and the prosecution had conducted the case and felt that he had been very hardly done by. For him the fight was by no means over.

Meanwhile, back in England, where there had been so much excitement at the goings-on in *Royal Oak*, the population had something more important on its mind – the Easter Holiday. As in Gibraltar the weather had been appalling. Now the weather forecast promised better things. Sunshine was forecast for the whole of the British Isles with only a cautionary note that the rain from Spain and the bad weather from Gibraltar might work its way across Europe. Already Weston-Super-Mare had a temperature of 60°F.

There were traffic jams on the coast roads and the railway stations were doing good business, but the real sensation was the number of people deciding to spend the weekend in Paris. Imperial Airways, flying from London's old air terminal at Croydon, had never had such an experience. Its bi-planes were taxed to their fullest extent. The company was laying its hands on any aircraft to be found. There were even cases of customers booking in advance! On the Thursday the usual three aircraft had been sufficient. But on Good Friday an unheard of seven were needed. Between 8 a.m. and 3 p.m. the unprecedented total of 85 passengers had been flown across the Channel. Another 82 were expected the next day. Commercial flying was catching on.

153

Britain was off on holiday – London Zoo, expecting a crowd and dubious about the weather forecast, had laid down new asphalt paths to avoid muddy feet – and suddenly, nobody had much time for the fate of quarrelsome naval officers.

Even the Mediterranean Fleet seemed to have lost interest. All through the day, while Dewar had been making his fervent appeal to the court martial, while decisions were being made and sentence passed, the ships of the fleet had been working their way to the outer bay. The flagship *Queen Elizabeth, Warspite, Ramillies, Valiant, Resolution* and even *Royal Oak* herself, all the great battleships had left their harbour berths. During the night they sailed, five days late, for their appointment in Barcelona.

It was very much a silent service once again. The Navy had had its fill of newspaper headlines and what went on when an admiral fell out with a bandmaster.

When Collard, Dewar and Daniel rose from their respective beds the next morning, the Navy had left them behind. And, for all they knew, for good.

15

'Why, it's Old Dewar!'

THERE WAS NO PURPOSE in any of the three naval officers or their families remaining a moment longer in Gibraltar than they need. The first thing that they did was to investigate liner sailings home.

Collard booked a cabin aboard the Orient Line's yellow-funnelled, 20,000 ton *Otranto*, homeward bound from Australia and sailing the following Sunday. Dewar, Daniel and their wives arranged a passage home on the same day, but, deliberately or otherwise, decided to sail in P & O's *Ranpura*, back from India on her way to London.

Life for the next couple of days, in that small social circle, particularly with the fleet away, must have been difficult, but somehow the Rear-Admiral and his two former officers managed to avoid meeting each other.

Then, on the Sunday morning when they were all due to leave Gibraltar, Collard performed a characteristically unpredictable act. Seizing some of the hotel writing paper, he wrote a separate note to Dewar and Daniel, saying he would like to meet them once more before leaving and inviting them round to the hotel where he was staying. He made sure that both letters were instantly delivered by messenger.

Dewar responded straight away. He immediately strode round to the Bristol Hotel. It was just about 9.30 a.m. when he arrived. Collard, who was sitting in the lounge reading a newspaper, leapt to his feet, extended his hand in greeting and, with a broad smile, cried, 'Why, it's old Dewar!' The two officers settled themselves down to a long chat, right until it was time for Collard to think about leaving for the harbour and boarding his liner. They shook hands sociably again on parting.

'So long old man,' said Collard.

'Good luck,' replied Dewar.

Their meeting was not unobserved. When the news reached the London newspapers there was many a sentimental, editorial pen. Soon the public were to read how the indominable spirit of the British and, particularly, of the Royal Navy, had shown through – good and honest men who bore no grudge nor malice in victory or defeat, although it is far more likely that it was just another example of Collard's ebullient nature, equally ready with a smile as with a scowl.

Unhappily for Daniel he had been out of the hotel when his invitation arrived. As soon as he saw it he, too, sped to the Bristol Hotel. But by that time Collard, his luggage and his entourage had departed. All that the Commander could do was to find some writing paper and leave a note of God speed to be forwarded.

The Rear-Admiral's arrival in England passed quite unnoticed. Not so that of Dewar. When the *Ranpura* berthed in London's King George V Docks quite a crowd had assembled. Dewar and Daniel, both in plain clothes, managed to slip ashore quietly. But stevedores, porters and crane drivers came running to Dewar's car. They mobbed it and then sent it on its way to a rousing cheer. Why he should have suddenly become some sort of a public hero it is hard to say, and the Captain was certainly not the man to want, let alone encourage, such a demonstration. Yet there it was and faithfully reported. It cannot have done his cause any harm at all when the Admiralty read its newspapers. And, judging by a leading article in *The Times* that appeared only two days after his court martial, he was going to need all the help he could get!

'Predominant over every opinion about the week's proceedings in court martial at Gibraltar, and about the incidents in which they originated,' it fulminated, 'will be a sense of relief and thankfulness that they are ended . . . an episode that has profited no public or private interest and remains devoid of significance for the life, organization and discipline of the Navy . . . regret and astonishment sharpened by impatience, that the elaborate ceremonial and procedure of naval justice should have been engaged by things of so little moment . . . We have Commander Daniel's own straightforward admission that it was a peculiar letter and that he exceeded orders . . . This peculiar letter Captain Dewar forwarded to the Vice-Admiral and admits that he did not disapprove it . . . Rear-Admiral

Collard, before the trials were instituted, had already been relieved of his command – a penalty which must be without parallel in the recent history of the Navy . . . The immediate upshot is that the careers of three officers of high professional competence have been interrupted, if not broken altogether, a result which again adds to the debits of this most unprofitable affair . . . an Admiral too much given to the choleric word, served by officers too dour or too zealous to keep the passing moment in reasonable perspective, too little gravity on one side and too much solemnity on the other, such seems to be the summary of an episode which has brought the Navy under the humiliating glare of unmerited publicity . . . which has made some ignominious and unusual events aboard one ship in the Mediterranean Fleet a topic for the world's discussion . . . everyone who knows the corporate spirit of the Service and the jealousy with which its good name is guarded will also know what it has had to endure in the indignities to which a malign chain of occurrences has brought upon it through no ascertainable fault of its own.'

If *The Times* and the Admiralty both felt that it was the moment for the *Royal Oak* and her courts martial to be swept under the nearest carpet, then they had no ally in Captain Dewar. It is clear that Dewar did not regard his passage home from Gibraltar as a restful cruise after the strain of the court martial, for the very day he landed from the liner *Ranpura* he fired off a seven-page, closely typed letter to the Admiralty, raising argumentative point after argumentative point, and with copious footnotes. He also protested strongly about the manner in which the courts martial had been conducted.

'During the first trial,' he wrote, 'the Deputy Judge Advocate was conspicious in his efforts to prevent the disclosures of relevant facts. His apparent bias against the defence was a subject of general comment and despite the dangers of such criticisms, *The Times* remarked on his attempt to dominate the court and counsel. That afternoon a certain gentleman (whose name can, if desired, be given in confidence) warned the Commander-in-Chief's secretary that the attitude of the Deputy Judge Advocate was playing straight into the hands of the Labour Party who would be closely watching the case.

'During my trial the Deputy Judge Advocate was much more careful but he made a remark to my counsel (not reported in the minutes) indicating that the words "Tending to bring into contempt" had been omitted from the second charge in order to secure a conviction. This indicated either an ignorance of legal procedure or a distinct bias towards conviction.'

157

Dewar's letter ended by accusing the Deputy Judge Advocate of prejudging the case and failing to show impartiality.

Enough work for one's first day on setting foot back in England? Not at all. The moment Dewar's car took him home to Kent, he was at his typewriter again.

Branksome,

Sevenoaks,

12th April, 1928.

'Sir,

With reference to the statement alleged to have been made by me in the *Evening Standard* of Monday, April 9th, I have the honour to report that I have made no statement, nor have I granted any interview, on the subject of the recent court-martial. I did, however, on the day after the court martial, say to *The Times* correspondent that I regretted the scandal which this case had brought on the Navy and that I hoped it would be allowed to die down as soon as possible.

I have the honour to be,

Your obedient servant,

K. Dewar.

The Secretary of the Admiralty.

(Copies to Naval Secretary,

1st Sea Lord and 2nd Sea Lord.)'

Sometimes the Admiralty had occasion to sigh!

On Monday morning, 16 April, 1928, the Board of Admiralty met. They were attended by the head of the naval legal department and the Judge Advocate of the Fleet. The only subject on the agenda was a review of the *Royal Oak* courts martial. It was quite sufficient.

C.M. Pitman, KC, the Judge Advocate, had by this time studied the minutes of the courts martial and also Dewar's letter. His report to the Board was enlightening. He said that he still felt the doubts that he had held originally about the second charge against Dewar and the equivalent charge in Daniel's case. It was his opinion that the court martial board was right to acquit Dewar in that instance. Consequently it must be held that the same charge against Daniel was not satisfactorily proved. The question of the sentences gave him much more anxiety although they were in due form and within the power of the courts.

'The accused,' he reported, 'appear to me to have conducted the defence on most injudicious lines. They insisted on cross-examining the Rear-Admiral and on tendering evidence which involved the court in an inquiry into the whole of the surrounding circumstances. They made it their object to convince the courts that their whole attitude towards the Admiral was justified, and it may well be that the courts, without so intending, really punished them for the way in which they conducted their defence, rather than for the actual offences of which they were convicted.

'There can be no doubt that the conduct of the Rear-Admiral was very bad, and when these proceedings were instituted I thought that a skilful and respectful defence would say "We were quite entitled to make complaints of such intolerable conduct, and, if our complaint did go beyond what was right, it was a technical offence which we regret". I anticipated that such a defence would result in a reprimand or possibly even in an acquittal.'

Although Dewar and Daniel would have been in no mood to admit it at the time, the Judge Advocate of the Fleet was turning out to be their own very best advocate.

He went on: 'Now that the accused have insisted on, and obtained, a full inquiry into the whole of their conduct in relation to the Rear-Admiral, the question remains as to whether they ought to suffer the full consequences of a sentence which appears to me to be based on their whole conduct, including the conduct of their defence, rather than on the offences of which they have been convicted.

'From a legal point of view there is no fault to be found with the sentences, but I have found it right to point out to Their Lordships that there is sufficient ground, should they see fit, for some modification of the sentences, or of their effect on the future of these officers.'

It was right, he added, that Collard should have been cross-examined.

The Advocate General, the Royal Navy's chief legal advisor, ended his memorandum, 'I would suggest that the whole machinery for making and forwarding complaints should be reconsidered. The King's Regulations and Admiralty Instructions should make it clear what a letter of complaint should, and should not, contain, so as to remove from the Service any idea that to complain of a real grievance against a superior officer is to court disaster.'

After so much food for thought, their Lordships were then presented with another memorandum and a very different point of view. It was from Sir Oswyn Murray, KCB, Secretary to the Navy, and was concerned with the sentences passed on the two officers. It included the phrase, 'The procedure of complaint would be impossible in a disciplined service if the right to complain gave the inferior a right to write whatever he liked about his superior. There is a line to be drawn somewhere, between what is inadmissible and what may be overlooked, and this line does not seem to have been drawn with undue strictness in the case of Commander Daniel.

'If the court-martial sentence on Commander Daniel be confirmed, the question remains whether any further decision, e.g. as to not employing him any further, shall be taken and announced . . . Many people might feel that Commander Daniel is, to some extent, the victim of Captain Dewar's unfortunate exercise of his discretion.'

The memorandum was considerably stiffer concerning Dewar's behaviour: 'One of the main reasons why a commanding officer is given discretion as to how he will deal with a letter of complaint received is in order that he may provide guidance to a less experienced inferior regarding his action, and prevent him from infringing the regulations or putting himself in a false position. Where, as in this case, the commanding officer himself, and his junior officer had common grounds for complaint against the Rear-Admiral, it is thought that the proper course would have been for the commanding officer to deter his junior from voicing these complaints at all, and to take the whole matter upon his own shoulders. He should then have made personal representations to the Rear-Admiral, using his utmost efforts not to promote a rupture, but to restore harmony.'

(Dewar's views on the wisdom of making personal representations to Collard about virtually anything at all were well known to anybody who had heard his evidence in court!)

The Secretary's memorandum went on: 'Captain Dewar, on the contrary, encouraged Commander Daniel to include a strong complaint . . . and then enclosed this with the more guarded statement of complaints which he himself put forward, thus, in a way, using his junior officer as a catspaw . . . He [Dewar] showed a fixed determination to promote a rupture, which seems difficult to excuse seeing that the Fleet was due to leave for important exercises, the success of which should have been the thought uppermost in the minds of all keen officers.'

And, to show how quickly gossip travels, the Naval Secretary added another reason for what he regarded as Dewar's lack of logical reason for the action he took by referring to that handshake between Collard and his Captain in the Bristol Hotel in Gibraltar on the Sunday morning after the courts martial. As he described it in that memorandum to their Lordships: 'Quite a short interview since the court martial,' he wrote, 'is said to have been efficacious in re-establishing good relations between the two officers.'

Sir Oswyn Murray raised the question as to whether Dewar should be employed by the Navy any longer or should be put on the retired list. Murray's opinion was that there was considerable justification for retiring Dewar as unfit for futher employment, but he did warn their Lordships that if they took such a step then they must expect something of a public outcry.

By now both Dewar and Daniel were on half-pay – £1 15s. 3d. a day in the Captain's case and £1 0s. 8d. a day for the Commander. But Collard was still receiving his full income. This was due to the fact that he was still on foreign service leave. When the Board met that Monday morning, his leave had still another six days to run. Oswyn Murray told their Lordships that this fact was probably the reason that the public and the Press felt that he had received no 'punishment'.

'It is understood,' Murray reported, 'that the first Sea Lord is of the opinion that the defects of temper and lack of self-control shown by Rear-Admiral Collard make it impossible to employ him further as a flag officer.'

He went on to suggest that there were three options open to the Board: to put Collard on the half-pay list and leave him there with no further action; to allow him to retire voluntarily, or to retire him. In Murray's view the choice lay between either of the first two courses.

He ended his memorandum: 'In view of the objectionable comments made in this country and abroad, it is for consideration whether any statement made should not include an expression of astonishment that, in this case, there should have been such an unaccountable absence, amongst officers of high rank, of the good temper and level-headedness usually found amongst all ranks and ratings.'

After studying the memorandum, the Board then displayed that it had a mind of its own. Collard's behaviour, they decided, was the principal factor in the whole affair. He was to be sacked forthwith. One of the charges against Daniel had been brought wrongly but the other three offences merited the sentence that he had been given and it should stand. Dewar's sentence, too, should be confirmed. However, their Lordships unanimously agreed that, by this ratification of sentence on the two officers, they had sufficiently marked their sense of disapproval of their conduct. They decided that neither man should be precluded from further employment when a vacancy arose.

Finally, they would review King's Regulations and Admiralty instructions to see if there were grounds for amending the procedure of complaining about the conduct of a superior officer. This was in fact done, though, as one might well expect, the modification took a long time and considerable argument.

So when that Monday morning Board Meeting was over, it was clear that Collard had suffered by far the most severe punishment, a fate that the Rear-Admiral must always have feared, however bold a face he had always worn.

The Admiralty's next step was downright brutal. A letter was despatched that very same day to Vine Cottage, Collard's home in the Surrey village of Witley.

'Sir,

'My Lords Commissioners of the Admiralty have carefully considered the reports of the circumstances which recently led to your being relieved of your command as Rear-Admiral, First Battle Squadron, as well as the minutes of the courts martial held at Gibraltar, upon the conduct of the captain and commander HMS *Royal Oak*, on that occasion.

'The review of all the facts leaves Their Lordships in no doubt that these regrettable incidents were largely occasioned by lack of self-control and peculiarity of temper on your part. They have accordingly decided to place you on the retired list as from 22nd of April, under the provisions of the Order-in-Council of the 21st of April, 1922, copy of which is enclosed.'

Even though the wording might have been typical in its style to any government department of that time, or of any time, come to that, it was a particularly cruel farewell letter.

Whatever faults Collard possessed, he had given forty loyal years of his life to the Royal Navy, had risen to high rank and had shewn himself a very gallant officer. But there was no reference to any of this nor even a single word of regret.

Collard never from that day forward, right up until the day he died, expressed one single word in public of anger, justification or indignation. Instead, on the morning he received that letter, he behaved exactly as one might have expected. He packed his wife and baggage into his car, locked up his house and drove away to privacy and an unknown address.

No confounded reporters were going to ask *him* questions! Good friends, and he had those, kept his destination secret. The theory is that he went off to the solitude of fly-fishing. In which case, the trout needed all the help that Heaven could send them.

After the Admiralty Board adjourned its meeting it had two days or slightly less to prepare a statement for the First Lord, The Right Honourable William Bridgeman, to deliver at question time to an extremely inquisitive House of Commons the following Wednesday afternoon.

When he arrived at the House and took his seat, those two champions of the Navy, Commander Bellairs, the Tory, and Lieutenant-Commander Kenworthy, for Labour, were eagerly awaiting him. Bellairs opened fire by asking him if, in future, the Admiralty would insist on twenty-four hours' notice of a court of inquiry being given. Bridgeman waffled some sort of a reply that explained precisely nothing.

Bellairs persisted. Was the Right Honourable gentleman aware that Commander Daniel had stated that he had only ten minutes to collect evidence for his court of inquiry?

Bridgeman said he would deal with that in his answer to the next question. That question came from Kenworthy. He wanted to know whether Bridgeman had any statement to make concerning the courts martial of Dewar and Daniel and whether those two officers had received new appointments.

Bridgeman then, for the first time, announced to Parliament and the country the decisions the Board of Admiralty had reached two days earlier. Collard had been retired, the sentences passed on Dewar and Daniel would stand, but they would be considered for future employment when an opportunity arose.

When he had finished Kenworthy rose again. 'When the Right Honourable gentleman speaks of further employment for these officers,' he asked, 'am I to understand that that means further employment at sea? And is he aware that in the case of an officer of the rank of Captain Dewar, unless he gets in his seatime, further promotion in the Service is denied to him, and that it would therefore be possible for the Admiralty to employ him on shore and to cut short his career in a higher rank?'

Bridgeman replied that he was well aware of the situation, but he could not give an undertaking that Dewar would be employed because the number of vacancies was limited.

At last a highly intrigued nation, which, apart from its Easter holiday had been following the story of the Rear-Admiral, the Captain, the Commander and the Bandmaster with ardent interest, had heard the whole story – the first wild rumours of mutiny, the court martial evidence and now the confirmation of the sentences.

Bridgeman's statement to the House of Commons was the highlight of that day's parliamentary business. Waiting in the wings to be introduced as the new member for Linlithgow was a certain Mr Emmanuel Shinwell who one day would become Father of the House.

The Press totally ignored the arrival of Mr Shinwell. But it had much to say about the Bridgeman statement. *The Times* leading article growled, 'One regret will linger obstinately upon a stage otherwise empty, a regret that the steam-hammer should ever have been allowed to engage the nut.'

Reynold's Illustrated News, a left-wing Sunday newspaper which always bore over its leader columns the imposing if not exactly original slogan 'Government of the People, by the People, for the People', started off its main leader: 'Mr Bridgeman is a gentleman with whose sayings and dealings *Reynold's* rarely finds itself in complete agreement. The statement of the First Lord of the Admiralty as to the review of the *Royal Oak* courts martial, however, provides the exception that proves the rule.

'We congratulate the Admiralty on the way in which it has dealt with the affair. If the matter had been in our own hands, we should not have acted differently.'

The People, also an opposition newspaper, took a rather more scathing attitude: 'It is to be hoped,' its leader writer said rather nastily, 'that the Navy generally will have learned from the *Royal Oak* incidents how very unwise it is for all concerned to wash soiled linen in public.'

The *News of the World* took a different line. 'Thus ends,' it remarked, 'this storm in a teacup, such a storm as will occasionally blow while ships are operated by men and not by angels. Fiction has familiarised us with a world in which seamen add a little colour to life afloat by the use of language barred from young ladies' schools. Fact seems, in this respect, to square pretty closely with fiction . . . What concerns the public is that the discipline of the Fleet is as a rock, unshaken and unshakeable as Gibraltar itself.'

Every one of these leading articles was carefully cut out, studied and filed by an Admiralty at once rueful, red-faced and fervently wishing that *Royal Oak* and all mention of her and her officers had never been. Almost pathetically, every even half-way kind word about the First Lord of the Admiralty was heavily underlined.

Then, two days after Bridgeman made his statement to the House of Commons and the Service was beginning to believe that all would soon be forgotten, Commander Daniel chose to make a public announcement. He had decided to leave the Navy!

16

'I've Come to Give myself up'

DANIEL HAD MADE HIS MIND UP. 'I have been punished,' he declared, 'for putting on paper what, strictly speaking, should have been a verbal report in confidence to my Captain. I have ascertained today that as a result of the court martial sentence, there can be no prospect of advancement for me in the Navy.

'Therefore, as much as I love the Service, it is imperative that I should seek a new profession at once, for the cost of defending my honour has taxed my financial resources to the utmost.

'I appreciate the promise of the Admiralty of further employment, a promise which is most exceptional in view of the sentence passed on me, but I have to consider what that employment is likely to be, and I now know that it cannot be employment such as I honourably desire.'

Daniel had some logic behind his decision. It was a time of retrenchment and of budget-cutting in the Navy. Officers for whom the Admiralty could see no prospects were being axed and had to leave without any suggestion of the golden, or even silver, handshake that a future generation would be offered. As a commander he had accomplished the first great hurdle of rising from the ranks of automatic promotion on seniority to one of selection on merit. Now, however, he had the smear of a court-martial sentence on his record.

Of course Daniel was not to know of the decision at that meeting of the Lords Commissioners of the Admiralty when it was decided that both he and Dewar had been punished enough. Nor, perhaps, was he bright enough to realize that enough political commotion had been stirred to ensure that questions would most certainly be asked, both in Parliament and in the Press if he were not given suitable employment within a reasonable time. The day would most surely come when their Lordships could dispose of Daniel in any way they chose. However, at that moment and without a question, for some time to come, he was virtually impregnable.

If Daniel had taken advice on his decision to leave the Navy, then it was bad advice. He was only thirty-nine years old, had been in the Navy for twenty-five of them and had been a commander for six. He had won the DSO and had been described as one of the Navy's most brilliant officers of the younger generation. But it is most unlikely that he sought any advice at all. For there was that other Daniel, the man who fancied his hand with a pen, the man who was renowned throughout the Mediterranean Fleet for his talent at organizing splendid ships' dances, for writing brilliant scripts for ships' concert parties and for his eagerness at staging amateur dramatics. He had just received an offer from a national daily paper to be its naval correspondent, at a considerably better salary than the half-pay on which he was presently living.

In the fashion of a later day, when the capturing of celebrities who were in the news was to become a routine exercise in circulation warfare, the *Daily Mail* had the bright idea of 'buying up' Daniel. Its sister paper, the *Weekly Dispatch* proudly announced that from the following weekend he would write a series of articles entitled 'The Navy from Within'.

It went on to list the first six:–

Daily life in the Navy.

Battle exercises.

Training for war in a battleship.

Naval administration.

How the Navy has changed in the last twenty years.

Changes Daniel would like to see.

Hardly the sort of stuff to have the public queueing outside the local newsagent on a wet Sunday morning!

But the paper did point out that, apart from being an expert on naval affairs, Daniel would also be writing in the *Daily Mail* as an authority on rowing, rugby football and the theatre. The Admiralty studied this announcement with furious interest. Daniel, as we know, was now an officer on half-pay and, while anyone in such a position has a great deal of latitude to embark on all sorts of enterprise, there are limits. Article 17 of King's Regulations and Admiralty Instructions was carefully read and re-read and marginal notes were made, but it was finally decided that by writing on such things as daily life in the Navy, rowing, rugby football and the theatre, Daniel was contravening no law.

Sadly for Daniel, he was no journalist either. He was shed by the *Daily Mail* as swiftly as he had been appointed. But not before, in his usual impetuous fashion, he had committed an unhappy gaffe or two. The worst was when he allowed his sword, the one that had lain before him at his court martial, to be displayed in a Piccadilly shop window as a sales promotion for pens. The theme was that the pen, his latest career, was mightier than the sword. This display did him great harm, particularly among those naval officers who, up until then, had been in sympathy with him. After quiet but firm pressure, the sword was removed from the shop window.

When he left the *Daily Mail* Daniel became a freelance journalist, but with no greater success. He turned to other jobs, but fortune was never on his side and his health deteriorated. When the Second World War broke out and he was still young enough and possessed experience so badly needed, there came the chance for him to make his peace with the Navy, but he simply was not fit enough. The only glimpse of service life he had was as the commander of a local Home Guard detachment, training the local butcher, baker, and garage owner to defend England should the Germans invade.

That war over, he found his way to South Africa. From a commander in the Royal Navy he became some sort of shipping clerk. Lonely and unhappy, he died of arterio-sclerosis in the public ward of a hospital in Port Elizabeth in 1955.

Dewar behaved differently. He took the Admiralty at its word and waited on half-pay for a new appointment to come along, although he was hardly content, for he still resented the attitude of the court martial and the conduct of the prosecution. He remained utterly convinced of the rightness of his cause.

The new appointment was made in September, 1928. Only five months after being dismissed his ship, he was given command of HMS *Tiger*. True, she was the oldest battle cruiser in the Navy and was serving only as a gunnery training ship, but she would give him those vital seven months of seatime that he so badly needed in order to qualify for flag rank. By now Dewar was among the most senior captains on the list and it could be merely a matter of months before he was promoted to Rear-Admiral. The promotion came and, with it, an appointment as ADC to King

George V. But he would never have the opportunity of command again, for he was almost instantly retired. His flag would never fly at a warship's masthead.

Yet the fighting was not over for Dewar. In the general election of 1931 he stood for parliament as the Socialist candidate for Portsmouth South. He lost, but polled fairly respectably, well enough to encourage him to think of fighting the seat at the next election. Then, by one of those almost unbelievable throws of the dice, Sir Roger Keyes himself was adopted as his Tory opponent. Dewar loftily declined the chance of fighting his old master.

In the early 1950s Dewar was in action again, this time bringing a libel action over a biography of Roger Keyes, written by Brigadier Aspinall-Oglander. According to the book, Keyes had written that Dewar and Daniel had made improper use of their 'nasty parliamentary friends prior to their courts martial. Not only that, but also that they had been responsible for the leaks that had so stirred up the Press at the time.'

Dewar held that this was defamatory and in due time author and publisher apologized, made a retraction and paid costs and damages. For once the Captain had found the law on his side!

During the Second World War Dewar, to whom tactics at sea had always meant so much, never found a chance to exercise his theories. Instead he found himself employed at the Admiralty as an historian. The real prizes and honours that he must once have felt would come his way never did arrive.

Vice-Admiral Dewar (like Collard, he was promoted during his retirement) died in 1964 at the age of eighty-four.

Vice-Admiral Collard made no fuss and never aired his views publicly. It almost seems that he had made a deliberate attempt to be forgotten. He had retired to the country and that was the end of it. In 1939 he could have gone back to the Admiralty. Instead he joined the Observer Corps and spent his time spotting for enemy aircraft. In his off-duty hours he would go over to a local girls' school and instruct classes in house maintenance – electrics, plumbing and bricklaying. The stocky little Admiral, with his weathered face and limp, proved to be very popular. The war over and his wife dead, the Admiral spent his final years a solitary man with little more than a fly rod for company. No one knows what he thought of those events at Malta. If he was hurt – and he surely must have been – then he was far too proud to show it.

Three men broken, two completely. Three careers wrecked. And, however you care to look at it, all over a swear word at a dance.

Broken and wrecked might be overstrong words to describe the fate of a fourth officer, Sir Roger Keyes, the Commander-in-Chief, Mediterranean Fleet at the time. His career could never be described as in any way a failure, but there is no doubt he did not achieve the highest goal of all: the one he craved . . . First Sea Lord. And he could not help blaming the confounded *Royal Oak* business.

Keyes had every confidence in the world that he would be given the post a few months after his term as Commander-in-Chief was ended. It all seemed so splendidly organized. When Beatty retired, Admiral-of-the-Fleet Sir Charles Madden had been given the job, in the full knowledge that, because of his age, he himself would have to retire in 1929 just in time for Keyes's return from the Mediterranean. The *Royal Oak* affair and the way Keyes had handled it put an end to the scheme. At the Admiralty letters were exchanged, memoranda passed and there was much confidential conversation, little or none of it in Keyes's favour. It would seem that a more powerful figure had taken a hand in the matter.

On his return from Malta Keyes went to see King George V, as was the custom on handing over a fleet. 'The King asked me,' Keyes wrote afterwards, 'if there was any precedent in the history of the Navy for one flag officer hauling down the flag of another. I said I did not know of one, but I still felt I had done the right thing. The King was exceedingly nice to me, but evidently thought I had made a mess of things.' According to the unfortunate Keyes, the King would not let go of the subject for over thirty-five minutes. 'He tried to argue,' he added, 'that I had really made "a balls" of it. We talked that sort of language.'

The King had not finished with Keyes even then. Harking back to Malta, he said it was a pity that the Admiral had encouraged so many young officers to play polo.

Keyes fought hard to be First Sea Lord. He even drove to Chequers, the weekend home of prime ministers, to lobby the current incumbent, Ramsay MacDonald. For this he received a stiff rebuke from the Admiralty. He also saw a letter from MacDonald saying that the King had already signed the appointment of Admiral Sir Frederick Field, who was three years junior to Keyes on the admirals' list. MacDonald went on to say that he felt it injudicious to make the King go back on his signature.

So, instead of becoming First Sea Lord, Keyes was appointed Commander-in-Chief, Portsmouth, a splendid post that would have rejoiced many a flag officer. But, as far as Keyes was concerned, his career was merely moving sideways.

Eventually he decided that, if he could not take a hand in naval policy at the Admiralty, he would do so in another place. In 1935 he stood for parliament at Portsmouth and won. (Perhaps it was just as well that Captain Dewar did not oppose him.)

Keyes made quite a name for himself in parliament and continued to do so when he became a peer and went to the House of Lords. But he never forgot how close he had come to the biggest prize in his career and how the *Royal Oak* business had damned it.

It would be absurdly wrong to make Day Kimball, the expatriate American defence lawyer, another victim of that dance aboard *Royal Oak*, yet even his career took a strange and unfortunate turn. He became an alcoholic, fought it and recovered, never married but took a mistress instead. During the Second World War he became assistant judge to the supreme court in Bermuda. After that he returned to his birthplace in the United States where, sadly, he took to the bottle again.

There was one more victim. The life of Bandmaster Percy Edward Barnacle, Royal Marines, was affected just deeply as any of his senior officers.

Percy Barnacle was a shy and sensitive man, perhaps as a result of his experience in the orphanage. He certainly never got over his horrifying ordeal when he was trapped below decks in a sinking ship during the First World War. Giving evidence at both courts martial had been a torture to him. That was plain.

Three years later, in 1931, he left the Royal Marines to find work ashore, but he never lost touch with the Service or his music. He and his wife moved to Plymouth, where he became involved with the Plymouth Silver City Band and was once more connected with the Royal Marines, this time with the Commander-in-Chief, Plymouth's band, which rather discredits Admiral Collard's view of his ability.

Band music has always played a most important part in the life of Britain's miners and it was about that time that Bettshanger, in Kent, one of the best-known collieries in Britain, was seeking a new bandmaster. The band approached the Commanding Officer of the Royal Marine Musical School at Deal, only a few miles away. Without hesitation, he recommended that they approach Barnacle. So the retired bandmaster came home to his adopted county, the depot in which he had trained and a new task.

The band flourished and so did Percy Barnacle. He became a church-warden in Deal and raised a family, a boy and a girl.

Arthur, the son, grew to be a strapping lad, looming over his father's mere five and a half feet. When he left school he followed in his father's highly polished boots and became a Royal Marine. Not as a musician but as a member of a commando.

One day he was to discover, with considerable pride, what a close family sea life is and just how much his father was part of its legend. Long after the Second World War he and his commando landed in Hong Kong on exercises. They fell in on the parade ground for inspection by the general officer commanding the station. The inspection over, the commando marched away with the exception of Arthur Barnacle who had been ordered to stand fast.

The general approached him. 'Tell me,' he asked, 'are you really Bandmaster Barnacle's boy?' Then he wished him well.

The Royal Marines most assuredly look after their own.

Father Barnacle led a very full life. After years with the Bettshanger Colliery Band, he became an instructor at the Royal Marine Music School in Deal. As such he was entitled to use the Officers' Mess but it was only when his son became an instructor too and led the way that he would enter it. He felt he simply did not belong.

Percy Barnacle, who always called his doctor 'Sir', even from his pillow, the gentle orphan boy who never swore was obviously the very last man who should ever have been cursed by an irascible rear-admiral.

Percy's wife died and he grew frail. He settled down to live in an old peoples' home in Deal, close by the things that mattered most to him, his church and the Royal Marine depot.

One afternoon in 1979 Bandmaster Barnacle, aged 87, put on his jacket and set out for a walk to the depot. Although not far in the ordinary way, it was quite a distance for him in his state of health. He passed between the whitewashed pillars and the open gates and headed for the guardroom. The young corporal of the guard, as sharply creased, as smoothly pressed and as immaculately polished as any Royal Marine corporal of the guard could ever be, quite naturally did not recognize him and in a friendly way, stopped him.

'I've come to give myself up,' explained the small, weary ex-Bandmaster Barnacle. 'That court martial. I didn't want to give evidence against the Admiral.'

The young corporal was utterly baffled until Percy found the words to explain. Then he was kind and gentle with the old man, found him a seat on which to rest and a cup of tea for him to drink. After that he guided the old man on to his path home.

Bandmaster Percy Barnacle died five years later, in 1984, at the age of 92, the last survivor of all those involved in that scene on *Royal Oak*'s quarterdeck so many years before.

Remorse never left him.

By those words of his to the youthful corporal, 'I never wanted to give evidence . . .' Bandmaster Barnacle showed that he had far more common sense than Commander-in-Chief, Admiral, Captain and Commander, put together.

APPENDICES

APPENDIX I
CAPTAIN DEWAR'S LETTER TO VICE-ADMIRAL KELLY

SECRET

HMS *Royal Oak*
At Malta,
8th March, 1928

Sir,

I have the honour to submit the following letter in accordance with the procedure laid down in King's Regulations and Admiralty Instructions Article 9. I am extremely loathe to make a complaint against my superior officer, Rear-Admiral Bernard St George Collard, CB, DSO, but I have no alternative as his behaviour is calculated to undermine not only my own position but the general discipline of the ship which I have the honour to command. After careful consideration I have decided that this is the only course open to me and the incidents complained of are therefore described below.

2. At an evening dance given on board HMS *Royal Oak* on the 12th January, Rear-Admiral Collard threatened me in the hearing of several guests that if I did not make the Commander do his duty in introducing people to each other he would make me rue it.

3. As careful arrangements had already been made for all officers to take turns in doing nothing else and as the incident occurred during the first dance when programmes were being filled I submit that this complaint was quite unjustified and that the manner in which it was addressed to me was most improper.

4. Later in the evening, the Rear-Admiral sent for the Executive Officer, Commander Henry M. Daniel, DSO, and told him to clear the Marine Band off the Quarterdeck. He then walked to where the band was playing and, having called for the Bandmaster, proceeded to abuse him in front of the whole band, the gist of his remarks being that he had never heard such a bloody noise in his life and that he (the Bandmaster) was to be sent home. He also turned to the Commander and said, 'I won't have a bugger like that in my ship'.

5. The foregoing remark was not only heard by the bandsmen but also by several guests and next day it was common talk amongst the officers and men of the ship as well as among civilians ashore.

177

6.   Despite the unreasonableness of the demands the Rear-Admiral's wishes were instantly carried out. The Marine Band was dismissed and the Volunteer Jazz Band was summoned. It required a good deal of persuasion on the part of the Commander to prevail upon them to play and so avoid a disgraceful fiasco.

7.   While guests were leaving the ship at the end of the dance, the Rear-Admiral addressed me at the gangway to the effect that he would not have the Bandmaster in his Flagship and that he was to be sent home without delay. When I respectfully protested, the Rear-Admiral became excited and it was only with difficulty that another scene was avoided.

8.   The attack on the Bandmaster not only caused a great deal of discontent on the lower deck, but also intense disgust and indignation amongst the officers who had taken infinite pains in organising the dance under very great difficulties. On the following day the Bandmaster put in a formal request to be allowed to resign from the Service regardless of sacrificing pension.

9.   Whilst I was considering what action to take, the Rear-Admiral sent for me and stated that he wished to squash a complaint conveyed to him by the Chaplain that he had called the Bandmaster a bugger. The Commander was thereupon sent for and, although the Rear-Admiral positively denied on his honour having used the word, the investigation carried out on the spot confirmed most conclusively the statements in paragraph 4 of this letter.

10.   I finally decided that, provided I could feel assured that there would be no recurrence of such an incident, it would be in the best interests of the Service to avoid a scandal concerning a Flag Officer. I therefore felt justified in taking no immediate official action, but it was necessary to reserve to myself the right of referring to this affair if, and only if, any regrettable recurrence should take place. With this consideration in mind no question of personal apologies either to the Commander or myself was entertained, but I decided that the Commander should make the best redress possible to the ship on the Rear-Admiral's behalf, who agreed to give him *carte blanche* in conveying the Rear-Admiral's apologies to those individuals who had been insulted. I directed that, whilst endeavouring to preserve the dignity of the Rear-Admiral, the interests of the Service must come first.

11.   It was made clear to the Admiral that grievous harm had been done and that in future the ship would be my first consideration. I also protested against the threat referred to in paragraph 2 of this letter and pointed out the impropriety of finding fault with the Captain in public.

12.   Since the foregoing occurrence everything possible has been done by the Commander and myself to re-establish the personal prestige of the Rear-Admiral and these efforts had met with considerable success, but, to my great regret, another incident on the night of the 5th March has altered the situation and necessitated a definite appeal to superior authority.

13.   On the afternoon of that day the Rear-Admiral sent me a message that, if it was too rough for the barge to come alongside on anchoring, a Jacob's ladder, boat rope and yardarm group were to be provided at the gangway.

14.   The ship approached the anchorage at about 2045 stern to wind, with a following sea which was rather rough but nothing to prevent a boat coming

alongside, although I confess it did not occur to me that this would be attempted except head to sea.

15.   Before anchoring, I got a good swing on the ship with the engines in order to bring her quickly head to wind, but, before the cable had run out, I received a message that the Admiral wanted me on the quarterdeck. I at once went aft and found him in a very excited state about five yards abaft the davit of the port ladder where a number of men were working.

16.   He at once commenced a threatening and aggressive tirade, the main points of which were:

> (a) he could not get a single order obeyed in this bloody ship, no ladder, no nothing.
>
> (b) he was treated worse than a midshipman.
>
> (c) he would not stay in the rotten ship and would ask to have his flag shifted.

17.   The trouble was that the Rear-Admiral wanted to use the port accommodation ladder whilst the ship was still swinging fast, although he had specified that if the sea was rough he would use a Jacob's ladder which was ready to be put over the side. The officers aft had not envisaged any attempt to bring the barge alongside until the ship had swung nearly head to wind by which time both ladders would have been ready if required.

18.   I regret any inconvenience to the Rear-Admiral, but since the original programme had stood at 2300 for anchoring there seemed no reason to assume that there was sufficient urgency to neglect the usual seamanlike procedure of waiting until the cable had been veered and the ship swung sufficiently for boats to come alongside head to sea. Had difficulty been experienced in getting the boat clear due to the swing of the ship on to her, the responsibility would have first rested with the ship's officers who in this case had received explicit instructions from the Commander. I wish to point out that less than 15 minutes elapsed between the anchor dropping and the barge getting clear. When I returned to the bridge after the Admiral's departure the cable was being veered and it was not until 8 minutes later that I could give the order 'finish with main engines – secure cable'.

19.   In conclusion, it may be pointed out that there would have been no trouble and no appreciable delay if the ordinary procedure had been carried out, that is, if instead of the Admiral coming up and giving orders, it had been left to the Commander or Officer aft to get the boat alongside when the ship had swung and to report to the Flag Lieutenant when ready.

20.   I take particular exception to the fact that the tirade referred to in paragraph 16 was made in the close proximity of various ratings, some of whom must have overheard the remarks addressed to me. With regard to the statement that his orders are never obeyed, I submit that they were obeyed on this occasion literally and in spirit. On demand, the Rear-Admiral failed to show me any occasion when his orders have not been obeyed.

21.   The statement in hearing of ratings that *Royal Oak* is not fit to be the Rear-Admiral's flagship is a serious aspersion, even if made in a fit of uncontrollable temper. No ship is perfect, but I can confidently say that all my

officers have been energetically applying themselves for some time past in the task of ever improving the ship's efficiency. My task in exacting a high standard is not made easier by remarks which are calculated to hold me in contempt of my subordinates.

22. When the Rear-Admiral first spoke to me about the ladder I told him I would enquire into the matter. He replied, 'I should damned well think so and get the Commander's reasons in writing'. These reasons are attached and no comment on them appears to be necessary from me except that I personally confirmed the accuracy of the Flag Lieutenant's message as stated by the Commander.

23. On the following afternoon the Rear-Admiral returned to the ship at 1745. The watch was fallen in on the quarterdeck ready to work the derrick and hoist in the barge. Entirely ignoring the Commander, duty Lieutenant-Commander and Officer of the Watch, who were stationed there to receive him, he shouted for men to get down the ladder, attend boat ropes etc. After completing the disembarkation of his gear, he ordered the barge ashore and walked past me without returning my salute. His general attitude and demeanour had every appearance of a studied insult to me in the presence of a large number of officers and men.

> I have the honour to be,
> Sir,
> Your obedient Servant,
> (sd) K. DEWAR
> CAPTAIN

The Vice-Admiral Commanding,
First Battle Squadron.
(through Rear-Admiral).

APPENDIX II
COMMANDER DANIEL'S LETTER TO HIS CAPTAIN

HMS *Royal Oak*
At Malta,
7th March, 1928

Sir,

In compliance with your verbal orders I hereby submit my report of the events connected with the departure of the Rear-Admiral from the 'ROYAL OAK' on the evening of 5th March.

2. In the first dog watch the Flag Lieutenant reported that the Rear-Admiral required to leave the ship on our return to the anchorage and that he was arranging for the barge to meet the ship. He also delivered a message from the Rear-Admiral that he required me to have a boat rope, yardarm group and Jacob's ladder ready in case it was too rough to use the accommodation ladder, as he did not wish any risk incurred of the barge being broken up. The interpretation which I placed on this message was that immunity of the barge from damage was the primary consideration. I gave the necessary orders for the provision of the gear and for the requisite hands, adding orders for the provision of extra fenders, heaving lines, etc.

3. The Gunnery programme was altered and in consequence the time of anchoring was suddenly advanced two hours. This information was received at 1930 and I immediately sent the hands to supper.

4. I made inquiries from the Fore bridge whether there would be any choice of sides for the Rear-Admiral's disembarkation and was informed in the negative; that the ship would be letting go the anchor at 2045 stern to wind. The ship would presumably swing head to wind and accordingly (there being no choice of sides) I ordered that the starboard accommodation ladder should be prepared for instant lowering, but it was not to be lowered without my orders. This restriction was imposed because, in my judgement, it seemed likely to be too rough for the barge to come alongside the accommodation ladder, and in any case I anticipated plenty of time whilst the ship was swinging to her cable. I made it clear that the starboard accommodation ladder must be completely ready, and that the Jacob's ladder, boat rope, etc. were also to be ready either side. If any hitch occurred I

expected to be informed by the Officer in charge, Lieutenant Lionel H. Phillips, and I personally went forward to make arrangements for the freeing of the port cable holder which had jammed the capstan engine. For this purpose I used the remainder of the starboard watch and stayed forward in case of any mishap with the other bower anchor. As soon as any possibility of any such mishap had passed I turned to go aft, and whilst cable was still being paid out I received a message that the Rear-Admiral wished to see me. I went aft forthwith and on arrival on the quarterdeck found a great commotion at the port ladder. Lieutenant Phillips informed me that the Rear-Admiral had ordered the barge alongside the port side and that he was angry because the port accommodation ladder was not down. I told him to proceed with all possible despatch and reported myself to the Rear-Admiral. As ratings were close at hand I made up my mind, for reasons based on previous experience, that if the Admiral made any scene I should keep complete silence, reserving my explanation until later. The Admiral was indeed furious, asking me why the port ladder was not ready in spite of orders which he had given the Flag Lieutenant more than two hours ago and he concluded by ordering me to 'see to it myself'. I replied, 'Aye aye, Sir,' and took charge personally.

5. In a few minutes I reported to the Captain that the barge was coming alongside and briefly explained what had happened. The ship was now swinging to port, and although the port side was, for the time, the lee side, the ship was bearing down on any boat alongside the port side. It would certainly have been against my judgement to have used this side or the other side until the ship had swung nearly to the wind. There was considerable swell, a rather choppy sea and sufficient wind to cause white horses.

6. The disembarkation was, however, carried out without damage and the barge shoved off at 2115. (The anchor was let go at 2103).

7. I informed Lieutenant Phillips that I was satisfied with the way in which he had carried out my orders and that I took full responsibility for the arrangements which, as far as I know, were exactly as I had ordered, viz. starboard accommodation ladder completely ready for lowering, a Jacob's ladder, boat rope heaving lines, fenders and yardarm group instantly ready for either side, with plenty of officers and men standing by.

8. In the course of subsequent enquiries as to what led to the Admiral's fury, I learned incidentally that he had told the Captain in a loud voice and heated manner, in the presence of seamen, moreover, that he was fed up with the ship. My informant stated that he felt disgusted at what he considered was the insulting behaviour of the Admiral to the Captain, although he did not hear in detail the rest of the abuse.

9. This concludes my report on the events, but I consider it my duty to point out what serious harm is done by such incidents. On the last occasion great pains were necessary to restore the respect of the Admiral in public opinion of the wardroom and of the lower deck, and I feel confident that this has been achieved. This occurrence, together with and emphasized by the insult before very nearly 100 officers and men at 1745 yesterday, has had a very serious effect on discipline and morale. Among wardroom officers, those who had the

mortifying experience of witnessing these scenes are inflamed with indignation, and all officers are deeply resentful of the humiliation to which they see their Captain and their ship have been subjected.

10. I myself was not personally affronted by any words used by the Admiral to me, and my sole reason for representing this state of affairs is that I consider the morale of the ship the special care of the Commander; and I should be guilty of neglect and cowardice if I shrunk from asking that a protest should be made in the most generous but uncompromising way possible at your discretion. Apologies would serve no useful purpose, but assurance is urgently necessary that discipline, which must depend on respect for rank, will not be undermined in this way.

11. Moreover, I wish to draw your attention to the inevitable apprehensions which prevail concerning the forthcoming Admiral's inspection. The ship is discouraged. My recent appeal to look forward to the inspection, thereby making it serve a useful purpose for the efficiency of the Service, has been reversed by the anticipation of vindictive fault-finding.

I have the honour to be,
Sir,
Your obedient Servant,
(sd) H.M. DANIEL
Commander.

SIR ROGER KEYES' MESSAGE TO THE ADMIRALTY

MEDITERRANEAN MESSAGE No. 901
(How the Admiralty first heard of the *Royal Oak* affair from Sir Roger Keyes.)*

SECRET

On the eve of sailing for Gibraltar and the Combined Fleet Exercises, Captain K.G.B. Dewar, supported by Commander Daniel, both of *Royal Oak*, brought certain allegations against Rear-Admiral Collard – the Rear-Admiral, First Battle Squadron.

I delayed the sailing of the Fleet for fifteen hours and ordered a Court of Inquiry, composed of the Vice-Admiral Commanding, First Battle Squadron, the Rear-Admiral Commanding, First Cruiser Squadron, and the Rear-Admiral (D), which finds the said Rear-Admiral, Captain and Commander gravely at fault. I concur and consider it undesirable that *Royal Oak* should sail flying the flag of Rear-Admiral Collard or with either of the other two officers on board.

I had the intention of transferring Rear-Admiral Collard's flag to *Resolution* pending Their Lordship's decision as to his future. He pointed out, however, that, in view of the presence of the Combined Fleets at Gibraltar and the publicity his supersession would entail, he would much prefer to leave *Royal Oak* at once, and offered to resign his appointment if I considered that this would make the situation easier and was in the best interests of the Service.

I have a high opinion of Admiral Collard as a sea officer, and his services throughout the winter as President of the Tactical Committee and Director of the War Game Room have been of great value to me. Nevertheless, I consider

* This first official intimation of trouble in the Mediterranean Fleet was about as enlightening as a glowworm in a coal mine. All Keyes told their Lordships was that he had usurped their own power by removing a flag officer from his command and had sacked two other senior officers. No real explanation as to why. Beset by sensational newspaper stories of mutiny and such like and a growing curiosity in Parliament, the Admiralty had to bluff its way for the best part of a week until the very belated arrival of the officer bearing the full facts.

it is not in the interests of the Fleet and the Service in general that he should retain his command; I have therefore directed him* to strike his flag, and he will return to England overland.

I have directed Captain Dewar to give up command of *Royal Oak* and to return to England forthwith, in accordance with K.R. & A.I., Art. 241. He has requested a Court-Martial, but owing to the departure of the Fleet and the importance of removing him from *Royal Oak* at once, I have informed him that the question of his trial by Court-Martial will be decided by the Board.

I have ordered Commander Daniel home overland forthwith, as I consider it in the interests of the Service that he should leave the Station at once. It is thought from the evidence there might be difficulty in framing specific charges for trial by Court-Martial which would meet the enormity of the conduct of these two officers, but if Their Lordships decide that Courts-Martial should be held, it is requested that these officers may be sent to Gibraltar by 23rd March for that purpose, and that I may be given instructions as to charges.

I am strongly of opinion, however, that it is not in the interests of the Service to give these matters the publicity that a Court-Martial would involve, and I trust that, after reading the evidence, Their Lordships will concur.

I consider it very desirable that the present state of discipline in *Royal Oak* should be corrected at the earliest possible moment, and I have approved Captain D. Osborne of *Egmont* temporarily to command *Royal Oak*, and Commander Warren of *Briony* temporarily to relieve Commander Daniel. I request, for the same reason, I may be consulted as to the new Rear-Admiral, First Battle Squadron. Rear-Admiral Munro Kerr would in my opinion be suitable† and his Flag Captain should be one agreeable to him.

The minutes and finding of the Court will be despatched tonight Sunday in charge of an officer.

---

* Keyes originally wrote 'Approved his request', but for some reason had the words crossed out and 'Directed him' substituted.

† Keyes had his way. Kerr was given the appointment.

SOURCES

The Ministry of Defence. Naval Historical Branch.
Public Records Office (ADM 156/188) Naval Historical Library.
The National Maritime Museum, Greenwich.
The Meteorological Office.
The Royal Naval Museum, Portsmouth.
The Royal Marines, Deal.
The Wickman Maritime Collection (Malta)
The National Library of Malta.
Adventures Ashore and Afloat, Admiral of the Fleet Sir Roger Keyes, George G.
  Harrap and Co. Ltd. (1939).
Roger Keyes, Cecil Aspinall-Oglander, The Hogarth Press (1951).
The Keyes Papers, edited by Paul G. Halpern, Ph.D. and published by George
  Allen and Unwin for the Naval Records society.
Pack and Follow, Joy Packer, Eyre and Spottiswoode (1945).
The 'Royal Oak' Courts Martial, Leslie Gardiner, William Blackwood and Sons
  Ltd. (1965).
Grace and Favour, Loelia, Duchess of Westminster, Weidenfeld and Nicolson
  (1961).
My Naval Life, Stephen King-Hall, Faber and Faber (1952).
The Times
The Times of Malta
The London Evening Standard
The Daily Mail
The Gibraltar Chronicle
The Illustrated London News

INDEX